CW00815856

THE BASICS
OF DATA
MANAGEMENT FOR
INFORMATION
SERVICES

THE BASICS
OF DATA
MANAGEMENT FOR
INFORMATION
SERVICES

PETER G. UNDERWOOD
Professor of Librarianship, University of Cape Town
and
RICHARD J. HARTLEY
Lecturer, Department of Information and Library Studies,
University College of Wales, Aberystwyth

Library Association Publishing
London

Published by
Library Association Publishing Ltd
7 Ridgmount Street
London WC1E 7AE

First published 1993

British Library Cataloguing in Publication Data

Underwood, Peter G.
  Basics of Data Management for Information Services
  I. Title II. Hartley, Richard J.
  025.04

  ISBN 1-85604-052-6

Typeset in 10/12pt Times from authors' disk by Library Association Publishing Ltd
Printed and made in Great Britain by Bookcraft (Bath) Ltd

For
Shirley
and
Jennie
(who has endured much)

Contents

Chapter One

Data and management

1.1 Introduction

This book is an introduction to managing data. Why data should need management is an appropriate place to start a consideration of the topic.

The management of any kind of organization, social group or enterprise depends on data. Without it, decisions have to be based on intuition and there is no means of judging the effect of what is done. Libraries and information services are no exception in this respect but they have an additional responsibility: providing access to data and information is their business. The managers of libraries and information services must, therefore, not only be able to manage data for the benefit of the services for which they are responsible but must also know how to manage data on behalf of their clientele. Norton[1] has commented that the library should assume the role of 'consultant-at-large' to the organization which it serves, aiding its work by advising on the design of information systems and advising on information management, especially when new technologies are to be used.

Librarians and information workers in public and academic libraries have an additional role which they can play: providing guidance and advice to the many people who want, or need, to organize data. Students preparing essays and projects, people running voluntary organizations, people with hobbies: these are typical of the many groups who may ask for help.

This book will describe various ways in which microcomputers and suitable software can be used to assist in organizing data and will provide guidance which will assist librarians and information workers in helping others.

Although computers have been in use for organizing data for many years, a commercial market for 'information technology' products has only recently been established. Its development has been rapid and there can be few organizations which have not been affected by the use of one, or more, of its products. As in many such markets, the pace of development has been fast and many new products are launched each year. A glance at a popular journal dealing with the subject will reveal many pages devoted to advertising; the prospect of trying to understand what purpose the various products might serve, let alone contemplating the task of learning to use them, can become quite daunting.

Fortunately, the products can be grouped into a set of categories which are unlikely to change much because they represent the main ways in which data need to be managed. These categories can serve as convenient means of thinking about data management problems and trying to understand what purposes the range of products might serve.

1.2 Managing data: an example

Helping to run a voluntary organization calls for enthusiasm, the skill of diplomacy, and an ability to work with others. Not keeping people informed about the activities of the organization can quickly lead to discontent and a decline in membership. Yet, even for organizations with few members, the task of keeping in touch can become a large administrative burden.

Names and addresses of members and other contact information, such as telephone numbers, need to be stored and arranged so that the details of a member can be found quickly. Other information about membership may be added to this basic record: category of membership, range of interests, payment date and amount of subscription could be included. If there are only a few members it would take little time to scan through the file, record by record, to find details such as which members have failed to renew their subscriptions but, as the number of members grows, such a task will become irksome and prone to error. The accuracy and the value of such records will be compromised by poor facilities.

An associated task is producing a newsletter or other publication for keeping the membership informed. The editorial work can be very great, especially if articles and items of news are received from members. These may need to be re-typed and edited to a consistent form, then arranged in sequence for duplication or printing. There will be a need to type letters to contributors and others.

Most organizations need financial records to show how much in subscriptions and other money has been received and how it has been spent. As well as keeping such records in a ledger there will be a need periodically to 'balance the books' to provide a summary for the information of members. If the records are not kept up to date, there may be a loss of control of the finances of the organization.

Each of the circumstances outlined above represents one of the fundamental ways in which data need managing: maintaining a file of records, dealing with the presentation of written text, and maintaining a set of numerical data. These also represent categories of software which can be used for data management: respectively they are database management, word processing and spreadsheets.

There are types of software which encompass other, more specialized, aspects of managing data but these are usually founded on one or more of the fundamental categories just mentioned. For example, a voluntary organization might want to put on an exhibition at a local craft fair to draw attention to its activities. Specialized software for project management might be used to draw up a list of required resources and their present location and a timetable for organizing their collection. In essence, the software is being used to build up a database of resources and then present some of the contents in the form of a table, using techniques found in spreadsheet software. Although such software may be considered a derivative of the fundamental categories, it is convenient to consider it in separate categories because it deals with particular, and significant, problems of data management.

It must, of course, be recognized that the use of 'information technology' products is neither inevitable nor, in all cases, desirable. For a small organization there may be little money to spend on anything other than the immediate concerns of the membership. There may be an understandable reluctance to learn to use a new technology if the benefit will be very slight. It is as the organization grows that the problems of data management become increasingly apparent and solving them demands either an increasing amount of manual effort and ingenuity or a modest investment in resources for data management.

3

1.3 What are data? What is information?

Apart from providing an academic exercise, there might seem little point in examining the difference between data and information. The words tend to be used interchangeably, it seems, even in the professional press. If a distinction is drawn, it is usually to the effect that data represent a raw state and it is only when data are organized for some purpose that a body of information can be perceived. Passing this on to others can be thought of as adding to the body of knowledge; where wisdom lies in all this is a consideration best left to the reader. In this book no strict distinction will be maintained.

There is, though, an important point to be made: whatever the term used, the data or information need to be processed, arranged and presented in a suitable form if they are to prove useful. Some thought needs to be given to the means of organization and it cannot be assumed that the use of information technology will, of its own accord, yield useful schemes of organization. Large sums of money were spent in the 1960s and 1970s in developing complex 'management information systems' (MIS) using powerful computer systems. The purpose of MIS was to support managerial decision-making but the systems, for the most part, failed to live up to the promise, partly because the technology was still young and not sufficiently powerful and also because too little attention was paid to the way in which managers actually used information for decision-making. Instead, the architects of MIS concentrated on technical sophistication and elegance in design. This was a wasteful use of money: the massive and expensive computer systems remained largely unused because the systems could not provide information in a form which was acceptable. Effective data management depends on the application of suitable technology within a framework of user needs.

The same point can be made about the use of computers to support public services in libraries and information centres: the design of the systems must be appropriate for the needs of both staff and users of the services. One must also accept that user needs will vary, so systems should be designed to offer alternative approaches. Fortunately, many newer systems have been designed to allow a flexible approach, though it is still an area where considerable improvement is necessary.

In both aspects of data management, whether considering data

4

management for managerial decision-making or data management on behalf of library and information centre users, the methods of organizing the data will be as important a consideration as the selection of appropriate technology.

1.4 The role of data management
The work of managers has often been described as planning, organizing, coordinating, commanding and controlling. Although many librarians and information service managers would agree that elements of these activities can be found in their work, few would be happy with a description which is so austere. There is a temptation to develop a normative view of managerial work, to suggest that there is a list of activities which forms the proper work of a manager. A manager is, by this approach, recognized to be a manager because of the type of work that is carried out.

An alternative view is offered by considering the roles that managers can be seen playing within an organization. Three groups of roles have commonly been identified.

The first role group is concerned with making decisions. In this role, the manager is concerned with the development of the organization, seeking to improve the range and quality of its services. To do this, the manager has to consider how to allocate resources and the criteria for choosing one area rather than another for development, and needs to assess, from time to time, how effectively the resources are being used.

Secondly, there is the role of providing information. Any manager is, by definition, responsible for supervising the use of resources and is thus in a good position to collect information about their adequacy. Senior managers can make use of this information and can coordinate it with information from the rest of the organization to build up a fuller picture. They are also in a position to disseminate information through the formal and informal communication channels of the organization.

Thirdly, managers are involved with other people – staff, clients, competitors, providers of resources and so on. Leadership, liaison and social duties may all come under this role.

It is the first two roles, decision-making and information provision, which are directly affected by the management of data. A failure to provide information which is accurate, at the right time and in a form which is appropriate, will reduce the effectiveness of the manager. Kotter[2] has commented that without knowledge it is not possible to produce a good vision or smart analysis and without that ability businesses cannot survive for long.

Library and information service managers have the additional duty of ensuring that timely and accurate information is available for their clientele. The question of appropriate presentation is also of great importance if users are to find information acceptable.

Data management is at the heart of most library and information service work and the proliferation of information or knowledge resources makes it an increasingly important topic for all professional information workers.

1.5 Tools for the job
There is nothing new in the concept of data management, at least as far as libraries and information services are concerned. Any library, any organized collection of documents, is evidence of an attempt at data management. What *is* new is the emergence of a technology which is especially designed to help with this work. Information technology will not, of itself, manage anything: the range of tools to be provided has to be chosen with care and their uses understood, and then they must be applied within an appropriate context. Intelligent application of technology is the keynote of successful data management.

The microcomputer has become a ubiquitous tool either as a stand-alone system or as part of a larger computing configuration. A typical stand-alone system might consist of a workstation (keyboard, screen and processor), a printer, disk store (hard or floppy disk) and a connection to a telecommunications network, perhaps through a modem. The cost of such systems is well within the budget range of most libraries and information services.

The use of the word 'workstation' to denote the heart of such systems is increasingly found in the literature. Microcomputers have often been bought to provide word processing facilities and this is still a major function for them in many services. Word processing has traditionally been a task for secretarial and clerical staff; managers and professionals have comparatively rarely felt obliged to develop the requisite skills to become competent at using a keyboard. Word processing facilities were viewed as a direct replacement for typewriters with the advantage that text could be corrected speedily, reproduced with ease and stored for future use in a convenient form. The development of computer-assisted ordering, accessioning and cataloguing systems did little to change this perception because data entry was predominantly still the task of clerical staff who were trained to enter data prepared by professional staff on paper forms. Even the task of editing data already in the system would involve preparing a paper copy printout which could then be annotated by professional staff, the corrections and other amendments being made from this by clerical staff.

The major change in attitude came with the development of online information retrieval. In the earlier days of information retrieval systems, searchers would submit a request for a search, with an appropriate search strategy, on a form and the details could then be typed in by clerical staff. Searches would be submitted to a mainframe computer system in batches and the results be sent to the searcher. There was no possibility of interaction with the system as the search was processed and any alteration in a search strategy as a result of the output had to be re-submitted as part of another batch. The searcher and the information retrieval system were effectively isolated from each other. Whilst a search might take a few seconds to be processed by the computer, the conduct of the search could extend, as far as the end-user was concerned, over several days. It might be argued that there is some advantage in this: the prospect of delay would ensure that only end-users with 'serious' and important searches would be prepared to spend time in explaining what was required and special care would be taken to check the search strategy before it was submitted. On the other hand, experience with manual searching would persuade many professional information workers that the ability to change strategies easily and quickly is a vital component when conducting most searches. Searching is seen as partly a social process, one for which there are comparatively few firm guidelines, or rules, and for which success or failure may depend on the searcher's ability to spot quite subtle clues and convey these clearly to the end-user. Feedback between the end-user and the searcher is an important part, perhaps the *most* important part, of this social process and this should also extend to the link between the information retrieval system and the searcher. In batch-processed systems this link was largely missing or its potential use was hampered by delays.

The development of online information retrieval changed this quite dramatically. Looking back on the development of any technique, it is often surprisingly difficult to identify one factor or development which precipitates a step forward. Often, it is not a question of identifying the flash of inspiration which leads to a development but, rather, a question of recognizing a gradual accumulation of trends and ideas, technical and social progress, from which a new process emerges. In the case of online information retrieval, three technical developments were necessary before it could appear. The first was the concept of shared use of computer systems through timesharing. This enabled several users to make concurrent use of a mainframe computer. The costs of provision of resources which were expensive could thus be shared and more effective use could be made of the resources. In addition, the use of more powerful computer systems facilitated the development of direct interaction, or 'real-time' response.

The second development was to enable this use to be made from a considerable distance by connecting computers to telecommunications networks, either private or public. The familiar procedure of 'dialling up' the computer system was established.

Thus far, the facilities available offered access to large amounts of computing power but this was, in itself, of limited use to libraries and information centres. The essence of information work is the storage and retrieval of information and it is the third development, the production of databases, which has made the use of computers so widespread in this professional area. Early databases were seen almost as a by-product of the increasing use of computer typesetting for the production of abstracting and indexing services. Their true potential as replacements for printed services was quickly recognized, however, and companies, or 'hosts', were soon established whose business was the leasing of such databases to make them available for interactive use online, with access through telecommunications networks.

Quite apart from the development of the market, the reaction of professional information workers deserves attention. It might be supposed that, because typing was an essential part of using online information retrieval services, clerical staff would be expected to type in search strategies under supervision. There is little evidence for this, however; on the contrary, almost from the inception of online information retrieval it was assumed that the professional information worker would sit at the keyboard and do the work. Perhaps the profession instinctively perceived a parallel with searching a card catalogue: it would be unusual, to say the least, for a member of the clerical staff to be summoned for the express purpose of turning over the cards whilst the professional stood by directing the strategy! Gradually, many professional information workers have acquired sufficient keyboarding skills to enable them to conduct searches, often in the presence of the end-user. Thus, the link between the end-user, the enquiry and the searcher has been re-forged and it has become acceptable for professional information workers to acquire keyboarding skills or, at least, some familiarity with the layout of a keyboard. A number of software packages called self-tuition 'typing tutors' have been developed and marketed and most students will gain some experience of keyboard use during a course of professional education. At all levels of the profession the use of computers has become an everyday part of professional activities.

The trend in office automation generally is to view the microcomputer as a powerful data-processing tool which can be used for many tasks. The term 'workstation' is often applied to microcomputers which have sufficient power to run several tasks concurrently, offering a 'multi-tasking' environment for data management. Producing a report, for example, might involve word processing, the retrieval of records from a database, the processing of some statistical data and the presentation of the resulting statistics in the form of graphs. Using an early microcomputer system it would be necessary to undertake each of these tasks separately, assuming that suitable software packages were available, and then, by dint of scissors and paste, to assemble the final report. A workstation environment equipped with suitable software would allow the integration of the tasks so that data from the database could be combined with the text prepared using the word processing program; the statistical data could, likewise, be prepared and included. The workstation environment would allow these tasks to be carried out concurrently, often displaying them by dividing the workstation screen into separate areas known as 'windows'; at the appropriate point, work on the word processor could be suspended while a database search was conducted, the results then being edited and inserted into the report by reverting to the word processing program. At the same time, the statistical data could be being processed, the results being displayed in another window as this was completed.

In addition to this ability to run several tasks concurrently, the workstation environment is often enhanced with extra memory, a high-quality display where common functions are represented by icons, and alternatives such as a 'mouse' for some keyboard work.

Early computer systems often consisted of sets of terminals connected to a central processor. The terminals in such configurations could only be used for input and output to the central processor. The trend now is to replace so-called 'dumb' terminals by microcomputers which can provide some local processing power. This local processing power of the microcomputer could be used, for example, for input and editing of entries to a database held on the central processor prior to the entries being added to the database. A multi-tasking workstation environment for this type of configuration would be a useful extension of facilities, though it is likely that some workstations will tend to be used predominantly for a limited range of jobs.

The development of multi-tasking environments is a good example of the way in which user needs and technological development in data management have interacted. At the outset the market for microcomputers was quite small and they tended to be used for a small range of tasks by clerical workers. The emphasis was on record-keeping and administration. Gradually, as managers began to realize the importance of data for strategic management of their businesses, there was a growing demand for computer systems which could be easily operated by people who were not specialist clerical workers and which could be used for a variety of tasks. The growing power of the computer systems gave software suppliers scope to include new features which enhanced the utility of their products. Advertising concentrated on new features, speed of processing, versatility and ease of use. Whether the subsequent use of the software was sufficient to justify its purchase is an intriguing problem beyond the scope of this book.

Data management is an important task for any organization and staff need to be aware of the potential for using the various types of software which may be available. Staff also need confidence in, and understanding of, the potential of information technology for data management to allow them to advise users and help them to apply the techniques.

References
1   Norton, N. P., 'Power to the information professionals', *Special libraries*, **81**, 1990, 119-25.
2   Kotter, J. P., *The leadership factor*, Free Press/Macmillan, 1988, 19.

Chapter Two

Implementation

2.1 Project management

The task of implementing the use of new software can be very simple. All that may be necessary is to choose and purchase the software, install it on a computer and then learn to use it. If the software is to be used by one person only and is intended to cover a single application there may be little need to spend a long time over this. Planning is confined to making sure the necessary funds for purchase have been made available and that a suitable period of time has been allotted for the tasks of installation and self-instruction; there is little need for further complication.

However, it is more likely that such software will be used by several people. There will, almost certainly, be several views on the choice of software; in particular there may be differences of opinion on what features are desirable and appropriate. Chapter Six discusses choice of software and outlines a practical approach to starting a project; this chapter is concerned with the overall considerations of managing the development of software resources.

It is advisable for one person to be responsible for overviewing development. This does not mean that one person has to undertake all the tasks of implementing the software; sharing and delegation of tasks are certainly possible and, in the case of a large pool of resources, may be necessary. Such division of tasks should, however, be coordinated by one person, who can act as a central source of information, initiate enquiries and plan training. The coordinator should be the channel through which enquiries are made to suppliers and comments about candidate software are brought together for review. Throughout the life of a software package on a computer system the coordinator should have a continuing role in being aware of new developments and the availability of new versions (often called 'releases') of the software. This need not be an onerous task: for most software there will be occasional releases of improvements and hints on better use. Information about these and, in the case of improvements, copies of the revised software are usually sent to registered users or included in newsletters. The function of the coordinator is to ensure that users are aware of the possibility of improved use and to assist in adjusting working practices to take account of these improvements.

The coordinator may, by choice or default, become an expert in using a range of software. This is a bonus and certainly helps to ensure that there is a strong motivation towards keeping abreast of new developments. It may be, however, that another user is able to take on this role, especially in relation to specific software packages. Essentially it is a role which develops and is recognized, rather than being assigned, because it depends upon the willingness, and ability, of a person to use and explore the capabilities of software quite thoroughly. It is the kind of role which is best spread through the organization because the concentration of expertise in one person can lead to difficulties if that person leaves or is unavailable. Expertise also offers a power base and a difficult problem can arise if the 'expert' chooses to release information only to a favoured few.

It is good practice to provide 'terms of reference' for anyone undertaking the role of coordinator. There is an understandable temptation in a small, close-knit organization, where people know each other very well, to forego this step and leave it to the common sense of the coordinator to carry out the necessary tasks and keep everyone informed. The temptation is even greater if the software intended for purchase is already well known or will only be used by a few people. In many cases no serious problems arise with this approach but there are significant risks. In the absence of terms of reference the assumption is that the person taking on the role of coordinator is fully aware of the background and circumstances of the organization, the objectives of the organization in relation to the project and the constraints which surround a solution. These matters may, in fact, be poorly defined or understood, even by quite senior people. There may be disagreement, openly expressed or otherwise, which may be a source of problems once the individuals concerned are faced with the task of making choices about lines of development. Therefore, even for an apparently small resource, it is wise to spend some time in exploring what functions the resource is intended to support and recording an agreement in the form of terms of reference. For the coordinator, too, the terms of reference form a vital guideline in that they should also specify resources available, constraints and reporting responsibilities.

Some caution is necessary when purchasing software. The computer industry, especially the microcomputer and personal computer sector, is fairly young. Standards are still evolving and are certainly not used by all manufacturers. It is quite possible, therefore, to find that software which has been written for use on a broad range of computers all manufactured to a supposed standard will not run without modification. Difficulty with output to printers and unexpected interactions with other programs are common problems which may be encountered when trying new software. This suggests the need to 'try before you buy', if at all possible, and, at the least, the need to have written confirmation from the supplier that the software is appropriate for use with the hardware and other software already in use. Such confirmation will be of help if problems occur and a legal remedy has to be sought. The legal maxim of 'let the buyer beware' is still good advice.

An orderly approach to documentation is also beneficial. Even quite small computing resources will attract and generate surprising quantities: statements of need, assessments of software, performance reviews, enquiries to suppliers and so on. These should be maintained complete throughout the life of software because they represent the decisions and the thinking behind those decisions; if there are queries or arguments about why particular actions have been taken this file could provide an answer. Once the software has been superseded or abandoned the file can be weeded of the less significant data such as preliminary enquiries and early statements of intent, but the information about the main steps taken should be retained. As information about new releases or improvements is made available this should be added to the file, together with a brief statement of action taken, and the file should be maintained throughout the time that the software remains in use.

With a small computing resource there may be a temptation not to plan for its use. In the absence of such a plan there may not be sufficient time available to install and become properly accustomed to the software. Good intentions to 'fit in' a day or an afternoon are no substitute for a plan which builds such activities into the timetable. The result of good intentions is often that notional time for familiarization is quickly absorbed by the need to respond to apparently more urgent needs; a partial familiarity is all that is gained and this is an insufficient base from which to set out to instruct others in the use of new resources. Installing computing resources is often a tedious and time-consuming task. The task of reading the documentation accompanying most hardware and software is often underestimated and, since few manuals are models of clarity, some experimentation will be necessary. Both jobs need undivided attention, so allow plenty of time for them.

2.2 Hardware

The pace of development in technology is such that new products are being released quite frequently. It takes some devotion to the trade literature to keep abreast of the developments and a good technical knowledge is needed to appreciate the impact of the improvements which each manufacturer claims to have made. The popular magazines which discuss and evaluate hardware and software are a useful first step because they often include introductory articles and clear explanations of technical terms. In addition, there are a few journals which are aimed at the library and information service professional: *Microcomputers for information management* and *Library computer systems and equipment review* are two that offer a good range of articles and reviews. Remember that some of the equipment described may be marketed under different names, or through different sources, depending on the country of origin. It is essential to check on availability with national suppliers and agents before designing systems which will make use of equipment which may have to be imported. Fortunately the market for hardware is such that innovations from one manufacturer are soon matched or even overtaken by the developments included by another.

The market is dominated by two broad ranges of microcomputer (sometimes called 'personal computer' or 'PC') equipment: IBM-compatible and Macintosh. The core of any microcomputer is the processor, which consists of a microchip. IBM-compatible systems make use of a family of chips produced by the Intel Corporation. The least powerful (and the first which were developed) are the 8086 and 8088 processor chips. More recent developments are the 80286 and 80386 and most recent are the 80486 chips. The development path is towards faster speeds of processing and the ability to handle data in larger chunks. Increasing the speed and power of a microcomputer system is important because the trend in the development of modern software is to include more features and to provide a set of integrated activities; if a reasonable response rate from the system is to be maintained then speeds have to be increased.

Macintosh microcomputers make use of the Motorola range of processor chips with the 68000, 68020 and 68030 representing the range in terms of power.

Co-processor chips may be an beneficial option, especially if software in which a lot of mathematical calculations are to be performed is to be run. Some machines include co-processors as standard but they can usually be fitted after purchase of a microcomputer if they are needed.

The quantity of internal memory (usually called Random Access Memory, or RAM) fitted to a microcomputer is of great importance, especially if several programs are to be used together in what is known as 'concurrent running'. The internal memory is used as a work space to store programs and data which are in active use. If several programs, or even one large program, are to operate then there must be sufficient memory available to support the processing. Memory is supplied in units known as kilobytes and all systems will be sold with a certain amount fitted as standard. The usual minimum amount supplied is 512 kilobytes (often described as 512Kb) but more recent models include up to 1 megabyte (1Mb). It is vital to check before purchase that the available memory will be sufficient to support the range of programs it is intended to run.

A microcomputer on its own is of very little use: it needs to be linked to other devices to allow commands to be input, data stored and retrieved and results displayed. The 'communication ports' fitted to a microcomputer allow links with other, 'peripheral' equipment to be made. Many IBM-compatible microcomputers include two types of port: 'serial' and 'parallel'. Serial ports are of particular importance if several microcomputers are to be linked together in a network and are also suitable for making connections to other peripherals which use this form of 'interface'. They are usually manufactured according to a standard, known as 'RS-232C'; in theory equipment using the same communications standard should be capable of exchanging data. In practice it is best to insist on a demonstration before purchase. Parallel ports tend to be used for short-distance connection to printers. Macintosh machines employ a different standard: the Small Computer System Interface (SCSI). This is a versatile standard which facilitates the connection and sharing of peripheral devices.

There are several ways of inputting data and commands to a microcomputer system. The commonest device is the keyboard using a standard layout. A layout similar to the order of keys on a typewriter is usual for the 'character' keys, though some interesting experiments with alternative orders have suggested that higher input speeds could be achieved, especially by non-expert users, with other layouts. It is possible to purchase keyboards with these alternative layouts (though they are far from common) and also keyboards with layouts suitable for languages other than English, including those using non-Roman characters. All keyboards will include additional keys, some of which may be used by programs for special functions. The configuration of IBM-compatible keyboards is often similar, although there may be a difference in the positioning of some keys and the 'feel' of keyboards is often quite distinct. Macintosh keyboards tend to be more compact than those of IBM-compatible machines and this may be an advantage if there is only a small amount of desk space available.

Keyboards arouse strong feelings in users. Some keyboards have a strong tactile response which may be liked by skilled users; others include features such as an audible 'key-click' which can give the user confidence that the keys have been depressed sufficiently. A useful feature is to be able to switch off such key-clicks since the noise can become irritating in quiet surroundings. In selecting a microcomputer system the quality of the keyboard is an important feature and one should certainly try it before purchase. If several machines are to be installed in the work place then the use of keyboards with the same layout is strongly recommended.

Two other input devices are commonly found. The first is a 'pointing' device consisting of either a ball mounted in a movable frame, known as a 'mouse', or mounted in a fixed frame, called a 'trackball'. Moving the mouse around on the desk, or rotating the trackball, results in a pointer being moved around on the screen of a display monitor. By 'pointing' to text or symbols on the screen and pressing a button or combination of buttons, a range of commands can be invoked. When combined with the use of the keyboard it is claimed that this makes the operation of a computer much simpler, especially for the new or occasional user. Here again, opinion is strongly divided: some users much prefer to type in commands and find the positioning of a pointer time consuming and difficult. New releases of software which support the use of a pointing device usually allow users to type in commands, if preferred. The best policy seems to be to allow users to discover which form of working suits them best.

The second device, not quite as ubiquitous as a mouse or trackball, is a 'scanner'. The printing of bar-codes on many products and use in systems such as circulation control for libraries and information centres has prompted the development of suitable readers. Early versions were fragile and unreliable. A more recent development in scanner technology is the development of 'page image' scanners which will allow the direct conversion of printed text into machine-readable form. An extension of this is a 'digitizer' which will allow other images, such as a photograph or a screen image from a modified camera, to be input to the computer in a form which can be displayed, modified and stored. There are exciting possibilities in using such devices for converting paper-based information systems, such as card catalogues, into machine-readable form.

The type of display fitted to a microcomputer is another area over which strong feelings are evident. The choice of display is critical to the acceptance of the system by users, so it is advisable to seek opinions as widely as possible. What appears clear and readable to one user may be distracting, or even distressing, to another.

Virtually all machines designed to be used on a desk make use of cathode-ray tube (i.e. television like) display technology. There is a choice between monochrome and colour displays and the quality of resolution of the display varies. There is also a need to decide whether graphic images, in addition to text, will need to be displayed. These options are determined partly by the type of cathode-ray tube fitted and partly by special circuitry, called a 'graphics adaptor' card, supplied with the system or fitted as a later addition. For a colour display the basic card is a CGA (Colour Graphics Adaptor) with a suitable monitor but the display can be difficult to read and work with, especially if used for long periods. Higher quality is possible from the Extended Graphics Adaptor (EGA) card, with the VGA (Video Graphics Adaptor) providing a superior display. Development of the VGA to provide a 'Super VGA' will lead to further enhancements. The best advice is to buy the highest quality display that can be afforded, especially if long periods are to be spent using it.

An additional display device which will be found quite useful if demonstrations to large groups are planned is a projector. This allows information to be projected on to a large viewing screen, often a similar type to that used with an overhead projector. The most convenient type is that using liquid-crystal display technology. The display is placed on to the projection screen of an overhead projector; the image projected on to the viewing screen may be somewhat faint and, for best results, the level of ambient light should be kept low. It may be difficult to display fine detail with clarity.

Printed 'hard copy' is often needed, especially to list the results of a process. The technology of printers has developed very rapidly and there are now several means of generating printed images. Important considerations in choosing a suitable printer are quality of output and whether continuous-feed (often called 'tractor-feed') paper or single-sheet paper may be used. Another consideration is carriage width, which dictates the maximum width of paper which can be loaded. Eighty-character is very common and will suit the use of the normal size of paper, A4. If it is intended to use wider paper, say A3 or A4 sideways, then a 132-character width printer should be chosen. Level of noise should also be assessed. This is of importance in a library or information centre because some printers produce a noise level which is irritating and quite intrusive. The use of an acoustic muffler, a large foam-lined box, may be necessary to reduce printer noise to an acceptable level.

Daisy-wheel printers produce a high-quality output, similar to that produced on a modern electronic typewriter. It is possible to change the style, and to a limited extent the size, of printing by changing the print wheel. The noise level can be quite high. Single-sheet stationery is normally used but the addition of a sheet feeder allows easy loading of a stack of paper rather than having to load each sheet separately. Tractor-feed may be fitted to most printers if continuous stationery, such as labels, is to be produced.

Dot-matrix printers are very common. At the cheap end of the market are printers with a 9-pin printing head. They are often used for draft printing but some can also be switched to a higher quality (but slower) correspondence-quality printing mode. A superior quality is offered by those printers using a 24-pin head and these can often be used to produce graphics as well as text. Such printers are more expensive and noisy but may be faster. The extra investment is worth making if the appearance of the output is considered important for the image of the library or information service. A recent development is that some are now capable of being fitted with a colour printing pack which uses a special ribbon. Dot-matrix printers are usually capable of being equipped to print on single-sheet (with the option of a multiple sheet feeder) or continuous stationery and may have 'paper parking' facilities which allow for changing from single to continuous feed by simply adjusting a switch.

Ink-jet, often called 'bubble-jet', printers are becoming more common and are coming down in price to the point where they are competitive with a high-quality dot-matrix printer, especially for use in administrative areas where the volume of printing is moderate and the demand for quality is high. They are quiet and are capable of printing on a variety of paper types in single and continuous forms. Colour printing is also available using a special printing head; the quality is high but the range of colours available is limited.

Laser printers offer, at present, the highest quality production of graphics and text though at a high price when compared with other types of printer. If desk-top publishing, with a mixture of text, graphics and illustrations, is to be undertaken then the purchase of a laser printer should be considered. The best quality is available from machines that make use of the PostScript page description language: this allows the output of very high-quality graphics and a wide range of character fonts.

There is a need to store data and programs: the internal memory of any computer is volatile and whatever is held there will be erased when the machine is turned off. In any case, the available memory will quickly be used up, even after a short period of work. Periodically, the contents of the memory, files of data and programs, are recorded on to some more permanent form. This often takes the form of magnetic disks. 'Floppy' disks are commonly available in 5¼-inch and 3½-inch diameters and with various capacities, often known as 'density' – as in 'single density', 'double density' and 'high density' – or, more precisely, in terms of the number of kilobytes or megabytes of storage. They are cheap and fairly robust but some care must be taken to keep them away from strong magnetic fields and very hot surroundings because exposure to those may lead to a loss of data on the disk. The disk drives fitted to the computer determine the size and capacity of disks which should be used. The great advantage of floppy disks is their portability: it is certainly possible to carry around, or even mail, copies of data and programs and, provided due care is taken in packing and carriage, the disks will survive unscathed. 'Hard' or 'Winchester' disks are fitted permanently to the computer and the disks are not usually changeable. They offer much higher storage capacities, of the order of many megabytes, than floppy disks and may be looked upon as a non-volatile extension of the internal memory of the computer.

Optical storage in the form of Compact Disc Read Only Memory (CD-ROM) has enhanced access to large files of data, notably bibliographic and reference material. At present this form must be regarded as a distribution medium for publishers; there is no feasible system, as yet, for recording a CD-ROM using the kind of computer equipment commonly available, though some experimental systems show promise. The great advantages of CD-ROM are durability and capacity: the discs are quite robust and storage capacities of about 700Mb are possible. To use a CD-ROM a special drive unit must be attached to the microcomputer and suitable software is used for searching the disc.

Access to large databases is also available through online information retrieval. These services are made available from large computer systems which are accessible nationally and internationally using the telecommunications systems, and which include telephone lines and special high-quality digital networks established for linking computers together. The distinction between these types is gradually disappearing as the ordinary telephone system is gradually upgraded to using digital technology. The connection of a computer to these telecommunications systems requires a 'modem', a device which renders the exchange of signals over the telecommunications systems possible by translating them from one form to another. Modems can be purchased as external units, requiring separate power supplies and cabling to connect to the computer and the telecommunications line, or they can be purchased as one of a range of 'expansion cards', designed to extend the facilities available on a standard microcom-puter. The use of an internal modem reduces the amount of space needed for the complete computer installation and reduces the amount of cabling since power and connections to the microcomputer can be supplied through internal connections. When purchasing a modem it is important to ensure that it will support data transmission at a range of speeds which is suitable for the telecommunications links and the computer services which are to be used. The speeds are quoted either in terms of 'baud rate' or 'bits per second', which is often abbreviated to 'bps'. The maximum speed normally available on modems used on microcomputers is 9600bps but the speeds commonly used are 1200 and 2400bps. Modems are used through a package of 'communications software' and it is important that the modem and the software operate according to the same communications standard. The most widely available is the 'Hayes' standard: all modems which are Hayes-compatible use the same set of commands for common functions. Modems are inexpensive components and most users quickly appreciate the advantages they give of access to external databases and a variety of other features such as electronic mail.

Within a building it may also be desirable to link microcomputers together so that messages and data can be exchanged and some devices can be shared. A Local Area Network, or 'LAN', consists of a cable circuit, expansion cards and network software. Several types of network have been developed and it is important to ensure that all components in the system are compatible. It will be necessary to install a cable circuit; this will need careful planning, both to ensure that its capacity is sufficient to meet present needs and allow for expansion, and to minimize the disruption to work when the circuit is installed. The cost will be substantial and a careful comparison of these costs with the anticipated benefits is needed before committing oneself to this development. If the sole requirement is the ability to share a limited range of devices, such as expensive printers, then a simpler and much cheaper solution is to purchase data, or 'T', switches which allow each microcomputer attached to the switch to request use of the device. If the device is free, access is granted; otherwise the request may be queued or denied. Data switches are not as versatile as networks and, in particular, will not support the sharing of some complex devices or allow many devices to be interconnected.

2.3 Software

The equipment described will be of little use without appropriate software. Chapter Six discusses the factors to consider in evaluating and selecting software and Chapters Three to Five are devoted to discussing applications and types of software. Before studying these, however, it is useful to know the main classes of software which will be encountered.

All computers need a major piece of software called an 'operating system'. Its function is to control the fundamental operations of the microcomputer such as initiating transfer of data to and from the disk drive, and transmitting characters to the printer. The operating system most frequently encountered in IBM-compatible microcomputer systems is either PC-DOS (Personal Computer – Disk Operating System), which is supplied by IBM, or MS-DOS (Microsoft – Disk Operating System) which is marketed by Microsoft and is usually supplied with IBM-compatible machines. Both types have been refined and developed over many years and several versions are in circulation. Although there is a high degree of compatibility between these types it is important to ensure that any other software which is to be used will run with the type and version of operating system in use. Macintosh microcomputers use a proprietary operating system, Apple-DOS. It is equally important, when selecting other software for use on the Macintosh, to check that it will work with Apple-DOS.

'Utility' software allows many 'housekeeping' tasks, such as file copying and erasing, to be performed more quickly or with greater ease than simply using the facilities included in the operating system. Utility software may also increase the range and type of tasks which may be accomplished. There are many types of utility software available and what, if any, should be purchased will depend on the frequency with which a particular task is undertaken.

The main purchase of software will be, in most cases, specialized 'applications' software. This is software which has been written to facilitate a specific range of jobs, such as storing and retrieving records in a database, word processing and facilitating calculations. The software may be acquired through a commercial supplier, in which case it will usually be necessary to enter into a licensing agreement if multiple copies of a program are needed to supply, say, several microcomputers in the same organization. It is a violation of the copyright law to copy software without having gained the necessary permission. If multiple copies are needed then either sufficient separate copies must be purchased or a site licence may be negotiated. This licence will allow the purchaser to make copies for internal use within the organization only. For a set licence fee the making of a number of copies will be authorized and multiple copies of documentation relating to the program will be supplied. It is important to realize, though, that such licences do not normally allow unlimited copying or the loan, sale or gift of copies of the software for use outside the organization. It is in everyone's interest to ensure that these arrangements work: if the software producers lose money through illegal copying (software 'piracy'), then they may be unable to fund further development of useful packages.

Another means of acquiring software is through the 'public domain'. Some software has been developed, often by interested individuals, and then donated so that it can be copied freely, without payment of fees other than the physical cost of copying. Typical applications are word processing, and database management. A slightly more restrictive version of this is 'shareware' where the producer, in exchange for the software, asks for a small donation, or contribution, to development expenses. In either case the costs will be substantially less than the price of commercial software. Shareware and public domain software may be good, well conceived, tested and a tremendous bargain for the library or information service with a small software budget; it can also be poorly documented, full of errors and lacking in any kind of support from the supplier. The best advice is to read the reviews of such software which appear from time to time in the professional and popular computing magazines and then to experiment. There are many very useful programs available and, although they may not be presented with quite the flourish and style of the commercial producer, they will do a very satisfactory job. Many commercial products will allow the same job to be done, and may offer more facilities; the intending purchaser should consider carefully whether such facilities will ever, in fact, be used. Sometimes it is the basic product, simple to use and uncomplicated to explore, which proves more popular than a much more expensive and ingenious package. Public domain and shareware products are listed in several magazines and there are groups which specialize in supplying them. Another useful source of information is on 'bulletin boards' run by various clubs and other groups and accessible through electronic mail.

There are some jobs which require the integration of several tasks. For example, it may be that one wishes to include a chart or a table containing figures in a document. It would be useful to be able to construct the chart or table, perhaps to carry out some calculations and then to transfer the results into the document. It would be possible, of course, simply to re-type the results, but this takes time and could introduce errors. A better approach is to transfer the data from the one form into the other. For this to be done with ease, the use of an integrated package is best. Such packages allow the interchange of data between their various functions and usually have a common core of commands which remain the same whichever part of the package is being used. This helps the new user to gain confidence and encourages exploration of the available facilities. Integrated packages tend to be expensive and are 'memory hungry': that is, they often need a large amount of internal memory to run satisfactorily. Before committing the library or information service to purchase of an integrated package one should be convinced that its power will be used. A less expensive solution may be the purchase of separate programs which are capable of accepting data from each other using a common format, for example the commonly used 'ASCII' (American Standard Code for Information Interchange) format. Data exchange may, however, be more complicated.

Many applications packages are supplied to the user as so-called 'turnkey' systems. This means that they have been configured so that having turned the computer system on and loaded the software the system will require no other specialized computer knowledge or input to run successfully. The package has been written, in other words, for those wishing to minimize their need for technical knowledge. Suppliers of the large applications packages for libraries and information centres often choose this form because it is a strong selling-point and minimizes the anxiety of using a computer system for those many professional people who have no wish to become fully versed in the details of operating systems and so on. In practice, it is rare for a turnkey system (or any other system) to run entirely flawlessly throughout its life and some more detailed knowledge of the computer system may become necessary, if only to be able to describe the problem to the supplier.

A difficulty arises if a 'turnkey' system does not offer quite the range of facilities required or if some aspects of its operation are not in accord with the way in which the library or information service plans to work. One approach offered by several suppliers is to market software as a set of modules which are capable of independent use, sometimes called 'stand-alone' operation, and can also be used in combination. A library or information service can then purchase modules to match the range of services required. Another approach is to offer a basic system which can be 'tailored' to meet the exact requirements of the purchaser. This is often achieved by allowing the purchaser to adjust 'parameters' or to choose from a fixed range of options. The advantage to the supplier of both approaches is that the basic system remains the same, thus making it easier to maintain and upgrade the software and make corrections if errors are discovered. The advantage to the user is that the supplier should have a good knowledge of the capabilities of the product and it should have been tested thoroughly, especially if it has already been purchased by several users.

Occasionally very specialized needs cannot be met by any existing system and no amount of modification will produce a version which is satisfactory. It may then be necessary to commission the writing of a 'made to measure' piece of software. This is not something to be entered into without careful consideration of the costs involved, the time that such a project will take and the input required of the library or information service. A lot of information will need to be gathered to specify precisely what the needs are and the required levels of performance. The software will need to be tested thoroughly, both by the supplier and by the purchaser; problems and errors can be confidently expected and this will extend the time taken to develop a satisfactory program. A library or information service manager contemplating commissioning a specialized piece of software should seek advice before proceeding and should assess the experience of potential suppliers in developing similar packages, their success in keeping to budget and to timetable and in supplying a satisfactory package, and their reputation for maintaining software.

2.4 Getting things to work
Library staff will, almost certainly, be involved in the installation of the microcomputers. Even if a complete 'turnkey' system has been purchased there will still be decisions to be taken about placement of the hardware and choice of furniture. A coordinator is a great asset in keeping track of the many decisions which need to be made. If the microcomputers are being installed for public use, the coordinator, as well as serving as a source of information about how to use the equipment and software, can ensure that consistent policies about use are developed and promulgated.

Providing an adequate power supply for computer equipment can be surprisingly difficult. Microcomputer equipment is usually designed to run from a mains supply which is stable and not subject to fluctuations. Unfortunately, other equipment in the library such as fluorescent lights, lift motors and photocopiers may introduce minute 'spikes' on to the mains supply. These minute flickers are not enough to upset most electrical equipment but are often quite sufficient to cause microcomputers to 'lock up' and fail to respond. One solution is to install a smoothing device which will filter out these spikes. In some cases this will not be sufficient and a separate power circuit, solely for running computer equipment, must be provided. Another approach is to install an uninterruptible power supply (UPS), which provides for a smooth power supply and will continue to supply power from a set of batteries, for a short time, during power cuts. This will allow processing to be completed, files to be stored, and an orderly shutting down of the microcomputers to be done. The disadvantage is the expense, though the price of such power supplies is reducing; some consideration must be given to the intrinsic value of data which might be lost if the power supply cannot be guaranteed.

Static electricity and excessive heat can also cause problems. The human body can become highly charged with static electricity and if this is discharged on touching a piece of computer equipment it is possible for microchip circuitry to be destroyed. There are, however, comparatively few reported cases of this happening and the frequent advertisements about the perils of static build-up may be more to do with the wish to sell anti-static products than with real danger. For the cautious there are a range of anti-static mats, sprays and even a personal 'earthing' lead to drain static safely away. Manufacturers are usually aware of the problems caused by build-up of heat and fit internal fans to vulnerable equipment. It is worth checking that there is sufficient space around equipment for heat to be vented and that nothing is allowed to obscure or cover the vents.

A far greater danger to computer equipment is the coffee cup. The contents, with or without sugar, will serve to disable a keyboard or a printer if spilt on to them. Particles of food will quickly clog small electrical contacts. It is possible to buy transparent, flexible, plastic covers for keyboards and to install printers in 'hush' boxes, which also reduce their noise level. These approaches will reduce the possibilities of damage but the safest policy is to ban food and drinks from the immediate area of the computers.

2.5 Security
Both floppy and hard disks are vulnerable to mechanical damage and damage from strong magnetic fields. Because their technology is electro-mechanical and involves fast-revolving components operating

to very fine tolerances, there is the possibility of the occasional malfunction or even major failure of the disk drives. In either case the loss of some data is almost certain. If the first rule of computer use is, 'make sure it is plugged in' the second should be 'always make a back-up copy'. Although the loss of a file of correspondence may be a nuisance, rather than a catastrophe, the same cannot be said of the contents of a large database. The problem of making back-up copies is that it takes a lot of time, especially if the file is large, and is a rather tedious job. Fortunately the development of small magnetic tape units, coupled with software which can periodically 'dump' copies of files on disks, has reduced these problems. Back-up copies should be kept in a separate room and, if they contain data judged sufficiently valuable, extra copies should be taken and kept somewhere quite remote from the computer system. Should fire, flood or other disaster strike there will then be a chance that a usable copy of the data will survive.

No microcomputer installation should be without a set of utility software. The contents of the suite vary with the supplier but essential components are programs to help with creating back-ups, sometimes called 'archiving' programs, and an 'unerase' program to assist with the recovery of data which has been inadvertently erased from a floppy or hard disk. Other useful components are 'sweep' facilities which allow the movement, copying, re-naming and erasure of multiple files and a disk sorter which will re-arrange files into orders defined by the user. If the equipment is to be left running for long periods, then a 'screen saver' program is worth acquiring; this will blank the screen of the monitor after a short period of non-use, thus preventing the burning-in of images on to its screen.

Hard disks allow the storage of very large numbers of files. These are often grouped and each group is given an overall name called a 'directory'. There may be also be hierarchies of directories and sub-directories; remembering under which directory a particular file is located can become difficult, even if some consistent pattern of naming and storing files has been instituted. A useful utility is a 'navigator' which will display the contents of a directory in the form of a 'tree' and search for a file if given its name or part of its name.

Transferring data and programs by exchanging disks or 'downloading' from a data network makes any computer vulnerable to attack by computer viruses. These are small programs devised to take control of a computer system and disrupt its work, often leading to the permanent loss of data and, in some cases, damage to hardware. They are often buried inside other software and can thus be imported quite unwittingly by innocent users. There are several 'anti-virus' programs available which can be used to scan disks and disinfect them if a virus is found. Specialized circuits to detect and eliminate viruses are under development and these may help to eliminate this menace. In the meantime it is important that all disks used, floppy or hard, are scanned regularly using an anti-virus program. It is also important that the program is kept up to date because new viruses are circulated from time to time and an older version of an anti-virus program may not necessarily detect newer versions of the viruses. If, despite these measures, a computer does become infected, the virus may show itself by bizarre messages or other curious screen images, and by loss of data. It is vital that the machine is isolated immediately from any contact with a network, and disks used with it should not be transferred to other machines until the virus has been identified and eliminated. The anti-virus checks should then be extended to the other computers in the organization to ensure that the virus has not already been inadvertently transferred. The danger is greatest whenever disks or data from outside the organization are used; software or data acquired from a reputable source should be 'clean' but it is best not to assume that this will be so. Microcomputers which are on public access will be especially vulnerable to infection and should be checked regularly.

2.6 Installing the software

A basic familiarity with the operating system (the DOS) of the microcomputer is essential if software is to be installed successfully. One must discover from the manuals supplied with the system or an appropriate published guide (which is often more intelligible) how to format and copy disks and how to set up directories and sub-directories so that programs and data can be organized satisfactorily. There is no substitute for time spent in the careful acquisition of this knowledge.

When installing new applications software it is usually best to read the instructions for installation thoroughly *before* commencing the job. The first step is often to copy the 'master' disks supplied so that, should some mishap occur, it will be possible to start again. Some software is supplied in a form which prevents copying, thus reducing losses due to software piracy but, at the same time, providing no recourse other than appeals to the supplier should some error in installation occur. The next step will vary. Some programs simply require the installer to type the command 'install', and the software does the rest. Others require the installer to set up a separate sub-directory and then copy the program and data files into it. The next step may involve configuring the program to run with the hardware, particularly printer type, and other software. This is usually the task of a special 'install' program which offers a range of menus listing different configurations from which the installer must choose the appropriate items.

Problems with installation usually result from some incompatibility between the operating system and the applications software, incorrect setting of internal switches on peripheral equipment such as printers or modems, or the selection of inappropriate configurations. It is always worth checking several times that cables linking equipment are correctly connected and running through the installation sequence before complaining to the supplier. Many run 'help' desks and will try to assist over the telephone. Another source of help and sympathy is a local user group; if one can identify a user with the same equipment this will often provide an excellent lifeline and source of support.

Good software is usually supported and maintained; it is practically impossible to ensure, even with a short program, that it will perform perfectly, and will be error free, under all conditions. From time to time new versions will be produced, often incorporating new features and correcting small errors. These versions may be supplied under contract to purchasers of the original versions or may be offered at a small cost. They are usually distributed on disk and installed either as a completely new program or in a form which will modify the previous version.

Some applications software includes a series of training files which demonstrate the functions of the program and allow new users to gain experience and confidence. They also provide an easy means of checking that the software is performing as expected, and a first check after installing a new piece of software might be to try such files out. Otherwise, it is best to check a new program with some typical data for which the desired output is already known: in this way, a simple check for installation errors can be performed.

It is worthwhile to keep a record of the installation procedure, especially if the local configuration requirements are special or have had to be discovered by trial and error. The failure of a hard disk drive may necessitate the re-installation of software and such records will save time and tempers.

Chapter Three

Spreadsheets

3.1 What is a 'spreadsheet'?

A large sheet of paper divided into rows and columns is called a 'spreadsheet'; analysis paper, often used for keeping accounts, is a familiar example. By labelling the rows and columns it is possible to record items and relate them to other items. For example, one could create a simple spreadsheet to assist with home budgeting: the columns could be labelled with the months of the year whilst the rows could be labelled with the sources of income and the types of expenditure and other outgoings which might be incurred. This is illustrated in Figure 3.1. Notice that it is possible to identify uniquely any portion of the spreadsheet by referring to the point at which a particular row and column intersect. Thus, the intersection of the 'February' column and the 'Food' row identifies one specific 'cell', containing the amount '£18.76' and representing expenditure on food for the month of February. A set of cells can also be referred to: the row labelled 'Clothing' identifies all the cells containing amounts for this type of expenditure for every month of the year. Similarly, the column headed 'March' contains all the cells recording financial

	JAN	FEB	MAR	. . .
INCOME				
Salary	1296.05	1250.47	1346.92	
OUTGOINGS				
Food	20.50	18.76	25.05	
Clothing	12.04	5.90	17.56	
. . .				

Fig. 3.1 Example of a simple spreadsheet

transactions for that month. The cells contained within the set formed by the intersection of the columns headed 'January' and 'February' and the rows headed 'Food' and 'Clothing' represent a block and this might also be considered significant for some purposes. Notice, too, that the use of headings allows a logical grouping of entries; all the 'expenditure' items can be grouped together, for example, so that they may be totalled up and the result subtracted from the income.

Each 'cell' can be filled in as the appropriate income is received or expenditure is made. Totals for the columns and rows can be calculated, providing, for example, an oversight of expenditure in January or the total expenditure on food for the year. As the spreadsheet is filled it becomes easy to compare the pattern of expenditure over several months or to compare the expenditures on, for example, clothing and food. It is also possible to calculate average income or expenditure, by months or type, and total expenditures each year or for shorter periods. Given a little familiarity with previous patterns of income and spending, it is even possible to fill in a spreadsheet for the following year showing the projected, or expected, patterns; this will provide a useful tool for forecasting and could help with planning the family finances. Using such a 'budget spreadsheet', if it appears likely that income will not equal the planned expenditure, the sums of money recorded in some cells can be reduced and the effect on the overall totals can be recalculated; the exercise can be repeated until a satisfactory balanced budget is achieved. Other strategies might be tested, such as delaying expenditure on some items until a time when extra income is expected, or the effect of using a loan might be tried. A spreadsheet provides a record of the past and a base for planning and forecasting the future.

A spreadsheet is useful for representing any data that can be sensibly organized in two dimensions (rows and columns); timetables, balance sheets, tables of statistics and records of events might all be organized in this way. Although spreadsheets are often used to hold numerical information, which can then be processed mathematically, they can also be used to hold other types of data which it is convenient to represent in a table. Names of people, departmental responsibilities and other kinds of textual data can also be included.

A spreadsheet is, thus, a very versatile tool which can be used in several ways for data management. At its simplest, it is a piece of paper and a pencil: this is often sufficient for small or 'one-off' problems. What, though, if one wishes to use a spreadsheet several times a day or over several months? What if one wishes to change the data represented in it quite often? What if one wishes to see the effect on the other data of changing just a few items? It is clearly possible to do all these things but the labour involved in making the changes and then performing the re-calculations by hand (assisted, perhaps, by a pocket calculator) may be sufficient to deter all but the most assiduous person.

The advent of personal computers has encouraged the development of many software packages providing spreadsheet facilities in a form which encourage updating of information and experimentation. These packages are usually called 'spreadsheet programs'.

3.2 What is a spreadsheet program?
Storing data, facilitating the entry of new, or revised, data and re-calculating the results is a task well suited to the use of computers. A spreadsheet program is a software package which allows the creation of a matrix of data locations, or 'cells' (this corresponds to a sheet of paper divided up into rows and columns) which can be labelled and filled with data or formulæ to be used to perform calculations on the data.

The first spreadsheet program was developed in 1978; it appeared on the market as Visicalc (visible calculation) and could only be used on the Apple II microcomputer. Despite this limitation the combination proved very popular, especially with the business community. Many other software suppliers saw that the potential market for spreadsheet programs was very large and that the developing microcomputer industry, coupled with the growth in small businesses, made it an attractive market. Several software packages, aimed at the same market, soon appeared. Supercalc began a trend towards designing programs which could be run on machines from several manufacturers which used the same operating system. At first this was the CP/M operating system, but the development by IBM of the PC, and the adoption of similar design standards by other manufacturers, meant that the MS-DOS operating system rapidly became the norm and several spreadsheet packages for this software environment have been developed.

Three main strands of development can be seen. The packages produced in the early years of development soon made an impact on businesses but users found that their use was severely restricted by the capacity of the spreadsheet. A limit of 64 columns by 254 rows was common and, although this sounds ample for all but the most complicated use, this proved, in practice, to be a considerable hindrance. Applications would have to be adapted to fit within these confines. The first strand of development has been to increase the capacity of spreadsheet programs and the modern versions available often have sufficient capacity to store several thousand rows and hundreds of columns. Limited capacity, then, is less of a problem than used to be the case but it is still important, when selecting a package, to check that its storage limits will not pre-empt development of a planned application.

The second strand of development is the range of functions. Early programs could do little more than perform simple arithmetic on columns and rows. This was adequate for uncomplicated applications and enabled one to produce balance sheets and tables of statistics quite easily. With a little ingenuity, formulæ could be devised using this small range of functions to carry out quite complex calculations. The mental effort, though, was often sufficient to drive users back to pencil and paper. The designers of spreadsheet programs quickly recognized the need for a number of 'built-in' functions and, just as with the development of pocket calculators, the range and sophistication of these is now a strong selling-point. Several offer alternative means of viewing results: the data in the spreadsheet may be viewed as a chart or graph, scaling and arrangement being decided by the user or determined automatically by the package. Using high-resolution displays and suitable printers it is possible to produce detailed graphical output, in colour, on paper or on transparency film for screen projection.

Having set up a spreadsheet, filled it with data and produced some results, many users then wanted to transfer data and results to other programs. A typical wish would be to transfer part of the spreadsheet to appear as a table in a report being prepared using a word processing package on the same machine. Early attempts at offering this facility were clumsy, necessitating the export of data from the spreadsheet to an intermediate format which could then be loaded as a file into the word processing package, finally to be transferred into the document. There was ample scope for error and the process was awkward and took a long time. The logical development was to produce a software package which integrated the activities of word processing, database management and spreadsheet use in such a way that data could be moved easily and with minimum disruption between these activities. The trend towards the adoption of such integrated packages is clear and several offer an extensive range of facilities.

3.3 Setting up a spreadsheet

The laborious part of using a spreadsheet program is setting up the spreadsheet. For anything other than the simplest application, one should spend time with pencil and paper planning the layout and deciding what cells need to be linked. Only then is it possible to define the formulæ. These should be tested on paper *and* in the working spreadsheet with data for which the correct answer is already known; in this way one can be reasonably certain that the formulæ, as defined in the spreadsheet, will calculate as anticipated. Most spreadsheet programs provide a set of 'ready-made' functions, such as 'sum', 'average', 'maximum', and 'minimum'; some provide chronological functions, such as 'date' and the ability to calculate the number of days between dates automatically. The functions provided in some programs include sophisticated facilities for financial and project control, such as 'Discounted Cash Flow' and 'Internal Rate of Return', which may be used in cells and as part of formulæ.

The 'ready-made' functions can often be 'nested' so that a succession of calculations can be built up, expressed in one formula and stored in one cell. There will be limits, arising from the program specification, to how many expressions can be nested and this should be checked before developing lengthy formulæ. There is a practical limit, also: an error in a long sequence may be difficult to discover. It is often best to break a complex formula into sections and store and display intermediate results, thus affording the opportunity to check that each section is producing the expected result. The checking of stages of calculations and results is vital but once it has been done, and the spreadsheet has been declared satisfactory, further checking will be unnecessary unless adjustments are made to the formulæ or to the structure of the spreadsheet.

Having decided on the intended structure of the spreadsheet, the next step is to transfer the structure to the program. Many spreadsheets provide a template several columns wide and several rows deep, whilst others will require the user to specify the required number of columns and rows for the spreadsheet, which will then be displayed. One must also make decisions about the desired width of columns: these can range from one character to the width of the display and may vary from column to column. It is important when selecting a width to allow gaps either side of data to aid readability. Most spreadsheet programs will separate cells by displaying vertical and horizontal lines but, even with this aid, values and formulæ can be difficult to read if they are bunched together. It is also important to ensure that columns are wide enough to accommodate the numbers to be stored. This may seem easy for data which are being entered from the keyboard because the user can readily see how much space a number will occupy. It is more difficult, however, for cells which are going to contain the results of calculations. Fortunately, most spreadsheet programs will display a code (often a row of asterisks) to warn that a column is too narrow to display a number; the result will not have been lost and will be displayed as soon as the width of the column has been increased sufficiently.

Another aid to readability is to leave an occasional row blank; this is especially useful if there are distinct categories of data which can be grouped together. Headings and sections of the spreadsheet can be segregated from the other data by using a row of hyphens or other textual symbols. Whilst none of these devices will change the use of the spreadsheet, they can certainly make a difference to the ease with which the data and results are read and interpreted. Some time spent on these features will prove helpful, especially if the spreadsheet is eventually to be printed on its own or as part of a report.

By using direction keys, or a mouse, it is possible to steer the cursor around the sheet. Positioning the cursor is aided by the display of column and row references at the top and left-hand side of the screen; the current position of the cursor is usually displayed as a cell reference (for example, C12 – column C, row 12) in a 'status' line and will appear on the spreadsheet matrix as a 'highlight'.

Most spreadsheet programs require the user to decide what kind of characters can be put into a cell: shall they be text or numerical? Textual data are used to label parts of the spreadsheet, whilst numerical data can be included in calculations. When entering numerical data, it is much easier to have labelled rows and columns with text identifying the purpose of each and this is usually the next job to be done. The text may have to be chosen with care because many spreadsheet programs limit the length of data which can be stored in a cell and, in any case, the number of characters displayed will be limited to the width of the column. Some spreadsheet programs provide character enhancement facilities, allowing the use of bold or underlined characters, for example; if the hardware and program have the requisite facilities, the judicious use of colour is another means of distinguishing parts of the spreadsheet. Most programs also allow the placement of text to be decided: left or right justified, or centred, are common options.

A spreadsheet may be wider or deeper than the screen can display at one time. This presents no problem for the computer, which will allow the display to scroll vertically or horizontally if a cell reference beyond the limits of the current display is selected. There may, however, be a problem of ease of use if the column or row headings have 'scrolled-off' from the screen. Faced with an undifferentiated mass of cells it may be very difficult to decide into which the next item of data should be put. It is possible to insert copies of the headings at suitable points but this will occupy more space in the spreadsheet and will give it an untidy appearance. A better approach is to make use of an option which many spreadsheet programs provide, 'windowing'. This option allows the relevant portion of the headings to remain on the screen whilst the associated set of cells appears in a window. The contents of the window can scroll vertically or horizontally and the headings will be adjusted to suit.

Another choice to be made is the format for displaying numerical data. A 'financial' format usually allows two figures after the decimal point and a comma separating the thousands from the hundreds and so on; a currency symbol may also be printed and negative amounts will be displayed within parentheses, for example, a substantial deficit might appear in the following form: £(1,012.13). For other kinds of numerical data it is usually possible to specify how many decimal places will be displayed, or to use 'scientific notation' which expresses numbers in powers of ten. The program may also include automatic 'rounding', which adjusts numbers to a defined length; thus, for example, it would be possible to set the rounding to one decimal place so that data such as 2.56 will be rounded up and stored and displayed as 2.6. The use of rounding is distinct from simply deciding how many figures to display. Rounding adjusts the actual value held in the spreadsheet; whereas altering the length of the display leaves the original number stored in the cell for use in subsequent calculations whilst a shorter form is displayed, for convenience, in the spreadsheet. For some calculations the most convenient form for both storage and display may be as integer values; that is, whole numbers not having fractional parts. The decision about number storage and display needs careful thought; some information is lost whenever the decision is taken to round or curtail the display, but the benefit may be that it is easier to perceive an overall pattern in the numbers displayed and to draw conclusions. The scale of numbers being handled and the sensitivity of the decisions being taken will often give guidance as to the precision with which individual elements of data need to be stored and displayed. For example, if one is trying to balance a budget of £100 the pence will be quite important, forming a significant proportion of the various sums displayed. If the budget is of several thousand pounds the significance of pence is much less. To include them might, in the latter case, confuse the user with unhelpful detail. Intended use may also be a good guide: a budget is not intended as a tool for indicating on what every penny will be spent. It shows the pattern of spending and helps the manager to balance the use of resources. A set of accounts, on the other hand, will reflect the actual pattern of spending in some detail and should show how every penny has been disbursed.

Having defined the width and format of a column, it is possible to use a command to replicate, or copy, the column once or several times. In this way the structure of the spreadsheet can quickly be built up. If, for example, 12 identical columns are needed for a spreadsheet divided into months, one can be defined and then copied 11 times. All that remains to be done is to add the names of the months. Some spreadsheet programs will even carry out this function automatically by allowing the user to specify the range of the desired headings and the required interval (January to December, one-month interval, for example).

The time taken to set up the spreadsheet may seem long but it will be re-couped when using and reading the results on the spreadsheet. Poor design leads to mistakes in entering data and in reading results; it is quite easy to adjust the design to facilitate use. An example of a poor design and an improvement is given in Figure 3.2. The poor design has narrow columns, just wide enough to accommodate the maximum length of numbers used; the improved design allows a gap either side of each number and this prevents one number from 'running into' the next. There is no heading for the table in the poor design; the heading should identify the purpose of the table and, if necessary, the period covered. The table is intended to record loan

	JAN	FEB	MAR	. . .
Granchester				
Adult loans	15045	16392	14850	
Junior loans	2039	2145	1986	
Melchester				
Adult loans	12960	10569	9986	
Junior loans	1045	1003	998	

Poor layout

Loan statistics for Barsetshire Libraries 1991

LOANS – 1991	JAN	FEB	MAR	. . .
Granchester				
Adult loans	15045	16392	14850	
Junior loans	2039	2145	1986	
Melchester				
Adult loans	12960	10569	9986	
Junior loans	1045	1003	998	

Improved layout

Fig. 3.2   Example showing two layouts for the same set of data

statistics from several libraries, each represented by the two categories of 'adult' and 'junior' loans; the poor design does not highlight
the names of the libraries so it is difficult to pick them out. The use
of indentation and spacing or, in more sophisticated programs, colour
and enhancing effects such as bold characters will serve to guide the
eye in picking out each group of statistics. These are quite simple
improvements but they will assist the user very greatly.

Many applications of spreadsheet programs consist of problems
which can be broken down into separate parts. By representing the
problem in the spreadsheet as a set of blocks of cells it is possible to
structure it so that the results from one block can be passed to
another as an intermediate stage in a calculation. For example, if the
total adult and junior loans for a county library service are being
represented, it may be convenient to group the individual libraries by
district, calculate and display the results for each district and then use

the district totals to calculate the grand total. The display of the intermediate totals also facilitates some checking to ensure that the calculations are being performed correctly.

Having established the outline of the spreadsheet, the next stage is to insert the formulæ. The purpose of the formulæ is to link cells together so that calculations involving data held in a range of cells can be performed, as specified by the user. For this purpose the cells are usually identified by a reference: the first column in a spreadsheet might be denoted as 'A' and the first row as '1'. To find the total of the contents of cells in column B of a spreadsheet which has data in rows 5 to 10, the formula might be 'sum (B5:B10)' (the exact form will depend on the program being used) and this formula might be inserted into cell B12. The formulæ usually refer to the contents of a cell by its reference; in this way it is possible to change the contents of a cell and know that any formula which includes a reference to that cell can still produce a result. Thus, in the example just given, it would be possible to alter the contents of cells B7 and B9 and then re-calculate the total. It would not be necessary to alter the formula because it contains cell references and not data.

Most spreadsheet programs will allow formulæ to be hidden from the user so that, on being instructed to calculate, the program obeys a formula hidden in a cell and displays the actual numerical result there also. The results of calculations performed elsewhere in the spreadsheet can be used in later calculations, if required. By linking formulæ together it is possible to create a spreadsheet which allows the easy performance of 'what if?' calculations whereby the effect of changing the values stored in some cells is determined and passed through the whole spreadsheet.

When developing formulæ it is important to have a clear idea of the exact sequence of calculations required and what intermediate values should be displayed. It may be helpful to describe the overall logic in words before attempting to translate it into cell references. Some users find it helpful to write a description using a kind of shorthand called 'pseudo-code'. This uses sentences such as:

annual total = Jan total + Feb total + . . . + Dec total
annual average = annual total/12

Once the user is satisfied that the formulæ make sense and will initiate the correct sequence of calculations, the next step is to translate them into the form used in the spreadsheet, using cell references to replace concepts such as 'Jan total'.

It is also important to appreciate the order in which calculations will be done if a complex formula is used. For example, arithmetical operations such as multiplication and division (often shown, respectively, by the symbols '*' and '/') are usually performed before addition and subtraction. So, for example, the formula

B3-C4*F2

will be evaluated by first multiplying the contents of cell C4 by that of F2 and then subtracting this product from the contents of B3. The formula will *not* be evaluated from left to right. Unless one is aware of this the results of a calculation may turn out differently from what is expected. Most spreadsheet programs allow the user to force a particular sequence to be applied, however. If, in the example just used, the intended sequence of events is for C4 to be subtracted from B3 and then the result to be multiplied by F2, the formula can be rewritten as

(B3-C4)*F2

The parentheses alter the normal sequence of processing and the contents are always evaluated first. If there are several sets of parentheses in a formula these are evaluated in a left-to-right sequence, so in the formula

(A2+C3)*(C4-D5)-F4

the contents of the first parenthesis are determined by adding A2 to C3, then the contents of the second parenthesis are evaluated by subtracting D5 from C4; next the two intermediate results are multiplied and then the contents of cell F4 are subtracted from this to yield the final result.

It is usually possible to have multiple layers, or 'nests', of parentheses and these can be used to build up quite complicated sequences of calculations. For example, the formula

(A2-(B3*(F3-(G4/G5))))

has the effect of, first, dividing the contents of cell G4 by G5, then subtracting this result from the contents of F3; this result is then multiplied by the contents of B3. Finally, this intermediate result is subtracted from the contents of A2. In other words, the innermost 'nest' of parentheses is evaluated first, followed by the nest which enclosed it and so on back to the outermost nest. The use of parentheses can clarify the logic of a complicated calculation and their use is recommended even when the normal order of processing will yield the desired result.

Formulæ can include constants as well as cell references; for example, a VAT rate could be included in some financial calculations or a discount applied. Using the range of 'built-in' functions and a little ingenuity it is possible to set up complex calculations and to pass the results from one part of the spreadsheet to another. It is vital, though, to test each formula to ensure that it does calculate as intended. Be wary, too, of unexpected events; a 'division by zero' error can be caused inadvertently if numerical data which would normally define the divisor in a complex calculation are missing or have been set to zero. Some spreadsheet programs provide facilities to test for this and similar problems and provide an early warning, but it is always wise to consider what effect the inclusion of negative values or zero might have on the success of a calculation. A little ingenuity may also allow one to build in some additional checks. For example, if row and column totals are calculated, the sum of all the row totals can be compared to the sum of all the column totals to check that all cells are included in the row and column formulæ.

Another useful feature is the ability to include a range of cells in a formula. It would be very tedious if, on wishing to add the contents of cells C4 to C9, one had to type a formula such as

$$C4+C5+C6+C7+C8+C9$$

Instead most spreadsheet programs allow the use of a built-in function, such as 'sum', together with the means of specifying a range of cells to which the function is to apply. The formula just mentioned could then be represented in a way similar to this:

$$sum(C4:C9)$$

The name of the function and the way of specifying ranges varies from program to program but the principle remains the same.

In this example the range is in one column. It is also possible in most programs to specify a row range (A8:F8, for example) and a rectangular range. An example of this latter approach would be

$$avg(C4:D6)$$

This formula would calculate the average value contained in the cells C4, C5, C6, D4, D5 and D6.

43

The more sophisticated spreadsheet programs will also allow logical operations such as comparing two values and selecting the greater. Conditional statements can also be included so that the contents of a cell can be inspected by the program and one of two possible formulæ used, depending on the value of the cell. For example, the statement

$$\text{if } C8=D4 \text{ sum}(C4:C6)$$

might be included as part of a formula in a cell. Its effect would be to prompt the spreadsheet program to compare the values stored in cells C8 and D4 and if they are found to be equal to add the contents of cells C4, C5 and C6 together, storing the total in the cell containing the formula.

Another function which is useful, especially if the spreadsheet is to be used for many 'what-if' explorations, is the provision of a 'lookup' table. This table is set up to hold data which will be used as a common factor in many, perhaps all, of the calculations. An example is the storing in a lookup table of rates of pay for employees where the scale point defines the rate of pay. If the spreadsheet entry for each employee contains a code representing the scale point, the spreadsheet program can be instructed to look up the scale point in the table, find the corresponding rate of pay and then copy this into the spreadsheet. One could, of course, do this manually when the data about each employee are first entered into the spreadsheet; the benefit of the lookup table method become evident, however, when the rates of pay for each scale point are changed as a result of a pay settlement. To make the appropriate adjustment for each employee by deleting the old value and entering the new is tedious; with the lookup table all that is necessary is to change the rate of pay for each scale point in the table. Any subsequent use of the spreadsheet program will result in a new rate being written automatically into the entry for each employee.

Despite having planned a spreadsheet with due care it is sometimes necessary, or desirable, to make changes. It may be considered helpful to the user to transfer a column or row from one part of the spreadsheet to another. Spreadsheet programs incorporate commands for moving a single cell, columns, rows and, in some cases, a set of cells. Perhaps an additional set of data must be incorporated or a new calculation made. It is fairly easy to adjust the dimensions of a spreadsheet by adding or deleting rows and columns and this can usually be done at any time during use. It is important to remember, though, that changes may alter the effect and range of formulæ: some spreadsheets will automatically adjust cell references included in formulæ to compensate for such changes, but it is always wise to check the integrity of the spreadsheet after making alterations.

Spreadsheets are often used for a period and then a new spreadsheet for the succeeding period is needed. One way of doing this is to design a new spreadsheet every time. It is also possible to take the spreadsheet from a preceding period, erase the data from the cells and use the framework again. Neither of these methods is really satisfactory because, in the first case, the labour involved in setting up and testing the sheet is fairly great. On the other hand, having to develop a new spreadsheet can give one the opportunity to incorporate new features or service developing needs. In the latter case, data from earlier periods are lost unless special efforts are made to preserve a copy. A better solution is to produce a 'base spreadsheet', or template, which contains all the row and column labels, formulæ and layout, but contains no data. Copies can be made as needed, thus allowing repeated use on successive occasions. Using the same framework on several occasions makes comparison easier, but one must be careful not to let such considerations become an excuse for inertia so that use of an inadequate spreadsheet framework persists long after it should have been revised.

A spreadsheet, once set up, is likely to be used on several occasions. It will probably, therefore, be stored on a disk until needed again. A spreadsheet may be used over a long period of time, also, with data being added to it from time to time. A budget, for example, may be set up in advance of the beginning of the financial year and then modified as actual expenditure replaces the projected expenditure recorded in the sheet. Over the course of the financial year data recording expenditure will be added and other data may be modified as it becomes necessary to shift patterns of spending to achieve a balanced budget. Thus the spreadsheet may be used several times a week, being retrieved, modified and then stored again on disk. The flexibility of the spreadsheet and the ease with which modifications can be made are considerable benefits but can also conceal a danger. It is all too easy to modify and delete data in error. All spreadsheet programs offer a means of editing data already in the sheet; some offer means of undoing a change just made. In addition, most spreadsheet programs offer a means of 'locking' or protecting data in specified cells or ranges of cells. This prevents the unwary user from adding, modifying or deleting data in the cells designated. A common use of this device is to protect the labels and headings used to identify rows and columns, but the principle can be extended to protecting cells containing values which change rarely, such as the rate of VAT. Another possibility is to extend protection gradually so that cells which have had data entered during the current session are then set to be protected.

Another aspect of protection is the storage of duplicate copies of the spreadsheet. Most spreadsheet programs are designed in such a way that when data are being entered, modified or deleted such changes are being made to a 'working' copy of the current file. If disaster strikes and some major error is committed it is usually possible to abandon the current session of editing and this will leave the latest copy of the current file unchanged. It is only on saving the 'working' copy that the current file is actually updated. One can extend this notion by using a facility built in to many spreadsheet programs, of automatically creating a 'back-up' copy which represents the previous state of the file, that is, the file before it has been modified.

Even with these facilities it is still wise to make a copy of the spreadsheet on a separate 'back-up' disk at the end of each session. There is a great temptation to omit this security measure; it often seems a waste of time, and can be tedious, but it is important to think of the consequences of losing the data held in the spreadsheet. Once the technology is familiar there is an understandable tendency not to keep many paper records, which quickly go out of date, because of the sheer ease and convenience of the spreadsheet program. The consequence of losing some data may be small: a matter of inconvenience but not a serious problem. Some data, however, are vital for day-to-day running of the library or information service and their loss would pose a serious problem for management. With such vital data one should plan for recovery from such a disaster and impress upon everyone the need to preserve copies of vital records.

The ability to 'protect' parts of the spreadsheet is important if the spreadsheet is to be used by other people. By protecting row and column labels and cells, or groups of cells, containing formulæ or values which should remain constant, it is possible to prevent erasure which might affect the integrity of the spreadsheet whilst still allowing users to add, delete and edit other data, perform calculations and print or display results. It is also important, however, to keep back-up copies of the latest state of the spreadsheet and the 'base spreadsheet' so that, should some accident to the working copy occur, it will be possible to resurrect or reconstruct the work. Now that many financial and other records are kept in this form it is hardly possible to over-emphasize the need for this and, in the case of vital records, the need for security copies to be kept, on disk and in paper form, somewhere remote from the working copy. Making a security copy should be a regular routine.

A printed copy of a spreadsheet is sometimes needed for reproduction in a report or because its contents need to be discussed by a group. A problem can arise if the width, in characters, of the spreadsheet exceeds the printing capacity of the printer. Many printers have an upper limit of 80 characters (at a pitch of 10 characters an inch), though 132-character width printers are now commonly available which allow printing on A3 size paper. Even printers of this capacity may be insufficient, however. Fortunately many spreadsheet programs have a range of character pitches which can be selected and one of these is usually a 'condensed' size. A very small size will make the spreadsheet difficult to read, however, and it is here that careful design will help to mitigate such difficulties.

Most spreadsheet programs will allow a portion of a spreadsheet to be printed and this will sometimes suffice. One approach to printing a large spreadsheet is to print it in sections on separate pieces of paper and then join the sheets together. This is far from ideal but sometimes is the only way of printing a very large spreadsheet. It is often worth examining the format of the spreadsheet carefully because there may be columns and rows which can be deleted or columns in which the width can be reduced. This may, of course, affect readability so some compromise may have to be accepted.

It is usually possible to improve the appearance of the printed version of the spreadsheet by including a heading, margins and borders. Whether it is worth spending much time on these features will depend on the intended use to which the spreadsheet is to be put. A sheet intended for external users may merit greater attention to presentation and layout than one which is to be used by staff. One should remember, however, that the layout and printing commands for the computer can be stored as part of the spreadsheet and will not then need to be decided on each occasion that the spreadsheet is printed unless the requirements change. Be prepared, however, to experiment; the appearance of data on the screen can be somewhat different from their appearance on a printout. It is often quite difficult to estimate printing positions and sizes of margins so several tries may be needed before a satisfactory printing layout is achieved. Time spent in designing a satisfactory printing layout is a good investment.

A specialized printing format is often included in spreadsheet programs which produces a printout of the spreadsheet 'model'. This represents the structure and layout of the spreadsheet but omits the data in the cells, with the exception of any constants, and substitutes the formulæ which are associated with a cell. It is also possible to display this 'view' of the spreadsheet directly on the screen; a printout is a useful permanent record for security purposes, however.

Sorting of data in a spreadsheet is something which may be of considerable benefit. The nature of the sort is usually defined by specifying a primary key and it is possible, in most spreadsheet programs, to sub-sort using a secondary key also. Thus, for example, it would be possible to sort employees by department and then sort the surnames of the staff of each department into alphabetical order. Another use might be to sort numerical data by size into an ascending or descending order. The range of the sort is also controllable so that only data within a specified set of rows would be sorted.

The user should remember that sorting will change the appearance of the spreadsheet quite markedly and it is also possible that instructions may be given in error so that the sorting has an unintended effect. It is advisable, therefore, to save a copy of the spreadsheet before attempting any sorting.

After the structure of the spreadsheet has been set up, the next task is to begin to input data. Many spreadsheet programs include an 'automatic re-calculation' feature which means that the program will re-calculate the result stored in the sheet every time a value is input or modified. This is useful if only one item of data is being changed but it can be most irritating, and time wasting, if this feature is allowed to operate when a long series of changes is being made. Fortunately it is a feature which can usually be turned off before the data are entered and then turned on again at the end. Should it prove desirable to re-calculate the results in the sheet before data entry is concluded, it is usually possible to invoke a command which will force a re-calculation.

Spreadsheets tend to occupy a lot of computer memory. Most spreadsheet programs display the amount of memory still available and it is important to check this display regularly. Running out of memory will curtail data entry but may also prejudice use of the spreadsheet because the computer system may 'lock up' and refuse to respond to commands. If memory is running short, space can be saved by deleting or shortening headings, deleting blank columns and rows, and reducing the number of intermediate results which are displayed. Once again, there may be a conflict with readability.

Another approach is to make use of a feature built into some spreadsheet programs which allows results from one spreadsheet model to be imported into another. Suppose, for example, a set of management statistics running back over many years is being compiled for a number of libraries and that the results from individual libraries are to be cumulated and incorporated into a summary. There is benefit in keeping such data together in one spreadsheet, but if the bounds of available memory are exceeded it would be possible to develop two spreadsheet models, the first recording the results from each library and the second calculating and recording the summaries. Instead of laboriously re-typing some data from the first spreadsheet into the second, one could save the intermediate results as a separate file and then load these into the second, summary, spreadsheet. It is even possible, with some spreadsheet programs, to have a dynamic link whereby changes made to the first spreadsheet will automatically be transferred to the second so that it will be updated.

The import and export of data can also be used to transfer data between spreadsheets, to help in building the framework of one by basing it on another. The scope of facilities for this depends on the program in use; some will allow the import of data from other spreadsheet programs so that data can be shared in an organization even though different programs are in use.

3.4 Choosing a spreadsheet program

Spreadsheet programs are a popular software package widely available for personal computers. Some, such as SuperCalc 5, are 'stand-alone' packages, providing facilities for creation and use of spreadsheets, printing of results and storage of data. Many will also allow results to be transformed into the form of charts and graphs.

Others, such as Microsoft Works, provide the additional benefit of an integrated environment whereby the results from the spreadsheet can be transferred directly to a word processor or database. The disadvantage of this is that some features of an integrated package may be more acceptable than others: one can like the spreadsheet, for example, but loathe the word processor. In addition, it may be difficult to justify the additional cost of an integrated package if separate programs for word processing and other activities are already available. An intermediate point is possible: some word processing packages will accept output from a range of specified spreadsheet programs and some spreadsheet programs may accept output from database programs but the file transfer routines may not be easy. If this is the chosen route of development it is important to check that the *version* and *release* of the software which it is planned to buy will be accepted by the word processing software. It is always best to insist on a demonstration using, if possible, local equipment and existing software together with test data typical of that which is to be processed; any problems of compatibility will then be revealed before purchase. Similarly, it is wise to check that the spreadsheet program will work satisfactorily with the printer, especially if unusual characters, or symbols, are to be included. Even the printing of common symbols, such as the sterling '£' sign, may cause problems with programs imported from other countries.

The capacity of spreadsheet programs varies considerably. Some will specify a limit by columns and rows; some may specify a maximum number of cells, allowing any combination of rows and columns. In other cases the capacity is governed by the storage capacity of the computer. Even here there are variations; for some the internal (RAM) memory is the limiting factor, whilst others set a lower limit. The capacity of cells may also be limited to a maximum number of characters. Careful planning and foresight is needed if a program with a capacity adequate for the purpose is to be chosen.

A feature of some more sophisticated and expensive spreadsheet programs, such as Lotus 1-2-3, is a three-dimensional structure whereby the spreadsheet can include several pages, each of which can be linked to the others or to specific parts of other pages. This allows, for example, a budget to be prepared on one page and the actual expenditure to be recorded on another, with the variance between projected and actual expenditure being recorded automatically on a third.

Check, also, the printing features provided, especially if output in the form of charts and graphs is considered to be an important aspect. The choice of styles for producing these – features such as automatic scaling of charts and graphs; a wide choice of shading, hatching and stippling; and, if supported by the computer, the choice of colours and hues – are important considerations.

The range of facilities offered by spreadsheet programs is wide and the selection varies from program to program. Most will provide commands to:

Add or delete rows or columns at any point in the spreadsheet.
Move the position of any row or column.
Alter the size of cells to accommodate smaller or larger portions of text or numbers.
Jump from one part of the spreadsheet to another.
Insert data, text or formulæ into a designated cell.
Fill cells by copying data or formulæ from one cell, or group of cells, to others.
Edit data or formulæ to correct or make changes.
Identify data, formulæ and text for particular purposes.
Designate the format of data to be stored in a cell; common formats are 'fixed decimal place', 'currency', 'time and date', 'text'. Data may also be aligned to right or left of the cell, or centred.
Protect the contents of one cell, or group of cells, from accidental alteration.
Clear the contents of one cell, or group of cells.
Calculate the value of formulæ when data are inserted.
Print a complete spreadsheet, or part of one.
Display results as charts or graphs.
Show the formulæ stored in some spreadsheet cells.
Make copies of the spreadsheet or the 'base' layout.
Save a spreadsheet and its contents as a file in memory or on disk.
Merge two or more spreadsheets.
Load data from other, non-spreadsheet, files.
View a portion of a spreadsheet; it may be possible to align one portion, or window, with another to facilitate comparison.
Search a spreadsheet for particular values, text, or formulæ.
Sort rows or columns of the spreadsheet into a useful order.

Some spreadsheet programs provide a 'calculator' function which allows results of simple calculations to be determined without the complication of setting up formulæ and entering data into cells. Another useful feature is the provision of a 'macro' function, which records a frequently used series of keystrokes and stores them under a chosen name; the macro may then be 'called' by name and implemented. It can be very useful: for example, one could create a 'search and replace' macro to find a specific value in the spreadsheet, replace it with the new value and then search for the next occurrence, continuing thus to the end of the spreadsheet.

3.5 Applications

A spreadsheet program is, after the word processor, the most widely used type of software. Several examples of use have already been given and its value when preparing financial statements or budgets must already be apparent. The ease with which the spreadsheet can be updated, the ability to recalculate when data changes and the facility of being able to try out different assumptions make it a valuable tool for financial control, the preparation of budgets and the allocation of funds.

Resource management has a much wider area of concern than control of money, however. Records of performance, such as statistics of use, can easily be kept and comparisons made with previous years to reveal trends and highlight anomalies. Given a long sequence of results, it is also possible to make forecasts, using the results of previous periods. Such forecasts can be valuable when preparing strategic plans and preparing bids for a change in resources. Caution is needed, however, in preparing and interpreting the results. *Any* forecast is risky and becomes riskier the longer the period into the future that the forecast attempts to project. Caution is needed to ensure that the results are interpreted in the light of common sense.

An interesting use of spreadsheets is in the planning of shelving capacity. Three approaches have been developed and are described by Auld.[1] One allows the comparison of five arrangements for an area of shelving using uniform shelf dimensions; the second predicts shelving capacities for five different arrangements with differing dimensions; whilst the third provides a means of estimating free shelving space over six ranges of shelving.

Auld also describes the use of spreadsheets to allocate staff to duty rosters, determine measures of productivity, and even record genealogical trees. This serves to demonstrate the versatility of the spreadsheet as a management tool.

Reference
1   Auld, L. W. S., *Electronic spreadsheets for libraries*, Oryx, 1986, Chapter 10.

Chapter Four

Databases

4.1 Introduction

Database packages are probably the most widely used type of microcomputer software other than word processors. Indeed, as far as library and information services are concerned, it could be argued that database software is the most important of all software types. In this chapter we explore the various types of software which can be viewed as database software; their differences are explained and the various uses to which each type of database package is best put are discussed.

The variety of applications of database software within library and information services is almost endless. In this chapter use is made of an example of a database developed by a public library for recording details of local societies, but there are countless other examples of database applications: the cataloguing of special collections, the operation of services for current awareness and selective dissemination of information services, a file recording borrowers, a file of addresses of suppliers and a list of contacts are merely a few possibilities. In all cases the common features are a need to store information about a person or a thing and a need to be able to retrieve information from the database for a wide variety of purposes. Thus the use of database packages is about storage and retrieval of information.

There are several types of database software, each having particular strengths and weaknesses. For example, the type of software known as a 'text retrieval' package has especially flexible interrogation facilities, whilst that class of package known as a 'database management system' is more likely to have good security features and data recovery procedures. Before considering the types of package in greater detail it is useful to consider some of the general features of a database.

A database can be viewed as any organized collection of facts although, as will be seen in later discussion in this chapter, the term has a much more restricted meaning when used by computer scientists. Whilst the term 'database' is most usually associated with computerized systems, it is perfectly possible for a database to exist in book or card or some other format. Thus, both the borrowers file of a library and the on-order file can be viewed as databases regardless of whether they are kept in a manual system – on cards or order slips – or in a computerized form. The information stored in the database exists to represent or, as many writers say, to model a real situation. For example, in a database of local societies, which might be maintained by a reference library, it can be said that the information kept about each society represents or models that society. Accordingly the whole database represents or models the societies in the given locality. It should be obvious that there are many different ways in which a local society can be represented or modelled. The exact representation which is produced depends largely on the way in which it is anticipated that the model will be used. In the context of the reference library, the 'model' of a local society is likely to consist solely of its name and the name of a contact person, address and telephone number. This is a far from complete representation of any given society but it is all that is necessary if the 'model' is built upon the assumption that the function of the database of local societies is to act as a referral source which can put enquirers in touch with contact persons in named local societies.

4.2 Database formats

A database contains information about those things or entities which it represents. This information is commonly referred to as the set of 'attributes' of the entity. The particular value ascribed to an attribute for a given entity is known as the attribute value. For example, a fictional database of local societies might contain the following information about a society:

Record number:	1234
Society name:	Aberystwyth Bird Watchers Society
Secretary:	Ms Sandra Higginson
Address:	252 South Parade, Aberystwyth, Dyfed, Wales SY52 9ZX
Telephone:	0970 123456

Meetings:	First Friday of the month in the Black Lion
Notes:	Regular trips to bird watching areas.
	Attempts to protect known breeding sites
	of Red Kites

The headings on the left-hand side represent the various attributes of the entity, 'a local society', whilst entries on the right-hand side are the attribute values assigned to this particular organization. Thus, a particular entity, the 'Aberystwyth Bird Watchers Society', has the attribute 'Secretary' and at the present time the name of the secretary is (or has the value) 'Ms Sandra Higginson'. It should be obvious that, unless there is some fairly drastic change in the structure of the Society, it will maintain the attribute 'Secretary' but that the secretary will change; that is to say, the attribute will remain but its value will change unless, of course, Ms Higginson is a particularly dedicated secretary! If the example of another society is considered, it should be apparent that it, too, is highly likely to have the attribute 'Secretary' and that it is improbable (though possible) that it will also have the value 'Ms Sandra Higginson'. Even in the unlikely event that the aforementioned person had tremendous energy and was secretary of several local organizations, there would be some organizations in the locality of which she was not the secretary. This discussion of the secretaries of local societies may seem somewhat protracted, but it is important to have a clear understanding of the difference between an attribute and an attribute value.

It is usual to organize the information in a database so that all the details about a single entity are stored in a single record, and each unique element (that is, 'attribute') of information which is stored is known as a field. Thus there would be a record for each local society or organization and the record would consist of several fields. Each of the various attributes would become a field within the record and it would be commonplace to refer to the names of these attributes as the 'field labels'. In the example above there are fields for 'society name', 'secretary', 'address', 'telephone', 'meetings' and 'notes', with these names acting as the field labels.

There are two common types, or formats, of record structure in existence, namely 'fixed field' format and 'variable length field' format. In the fixed field format, once the length of a field has been determined by the database designer, that field is of the same length in every record. This type of structure is more predictable and easier for the system programmer to cope with because the position of each field in each record will be known. It has the disadvantage that in those records where a particular field has a short value some of the storage space assigned to the field is, in effect, wasted. Conversely, in those records where the field has a particularly large value then it will be necessary to abbreviate the entry in the database. If abbreviation is necessary, the database designer/manager must decide between accepting the possibility that some of the data in the database may be stored and presented inconsistently, with consequences in the success of future attempts at retrieval, or accepting the additional overhead cost of some form of authority file to ensure that the abbreviations are consistently applied. The best solution is to seek some compromise by which the field length chosen is such that in most records the information can be accommodated whilst in a minority abbreviations are necessary. Place names provide an excellent example of the difficulties facing the user of a fixed length field format. Some place names, such as Tenby, are brief and consist of single words, but many are much longer, such as Llanfairfechan, or consist of several words, such as Llanfihangel y Creuddyn. To take the example of the place with the longest name in the United Kingdom, Llanfairpwllgwyngyllgogerychwyrndrobwllllantysiliogogoch, if the database designer provided a field length which catered for this there would be considerable waste of storage in the majority of records, in which the name of the place is much briefer.

The alternative to fixed length fields is to have a structure with variable length fields. In this type of structure, the beginning of each new record is tagged by a 'beginning of record' marker and the beginning of a field is tagged with a 'beginning of field' marker, each field having a different marker. The end of each field is signified by an 'end of field' marker. These markers must be characters which are unlikely to be used as a part of any record within the database: typically, characters such as '@' and '#' (hash). Obviously, this approach has the advantage that the data do not have to be abbreviated whilst it has the disadvantage that it becomes more complicated to enter and edit the data. Experience shows that many of the textual data with which librarians are frequently working are best dealt with by variable length field databases. The example of place name from a file of borrowers is but one example. The input of bibliographic details also offers examples where, for a given entity, there is considerable variation in the length of various attributes, such as title, names of authors and publisher.

A final option is the 'directory format' record structure. In this structure the start of each record is occupied by a directory, which can be viewed as being the contents page of the record. It contains pointers to the start of the various fields within the record. Thus, the record for the Aberystwyth Bird Watchers Society might look like this:

> 1/5/38/57/108/119/162@1234Aberystwyth Bird Watchers
> SocietyMs Sandra Higginson252 South Parade,
> Aberystwyth, Dyfed, Wales SY52 9ZX0970 123456First
> Friday of the month in the Black LionRegular trips to
> bird watching areas. Attempts to protect known breeding
> sites of Red Kites#

where the string of characters, 1/5/38/57/108/119/162@ constitutes the directory for the record and indicates the position of the starting character of each field. The end of the directory information is shown by the character '@' and this denotes the point after which the characters constitute the data held in the record. Each character position is numbered with reference to the end of the directory. The directory indicates the position of the fields within the data as follows:

Record number:	starting character position 1, following @
Society name:	starting character position 5
Secretary:	starting character position 38
Address:	starting character position 57
Telephone:	starting character position 108
Meetings:	starting character position 119
Notes:	starting character position 162

The end of the record is indicated by a 'hash' mark, '#', and the directory of the next record will follow on without break. By detecting these 'end of record' markers the computer is able to distinguish between one record and another and can count records to find its way around a database.

This type of structure can be used with either a fixed field format or a variable length field structure. The MARC (MAchine Readable Cataloguing) record structure, which is known at least by name to most librarians, is an example of a directory structure, although it is far more complex than the example which has been used here.

This consideration of formats serves to emphasize an important point which is often overlooked by those unused to the ways of computers. A human, looking at a record, can easily distinguish the different types of data stored therein: in the example above, the name of the secretary of the society is readily distinguishable from details of the meetings. Both, however, are represented by alphabetic characters and would be regarded as the same sort of data by a computer. In other words, a human uses context, form and other 'real world' information and experience to extract meaning. Although some progress has been made in designing computer programs which can apply sets of rules to extract meaning and make similar distinctions, it will be some time before we can expect that a computer system will be able to identify a name, place or other category of information in a body of text without use of formatting information.

Having once created a set of records in a database it is possible to use the formatted data in a variety of ways. To continue with the former example, it might be decided that a printed copy of the records should be created, arranged in alphabetic order by name of society. As a preliminary step, the database could be sorted using the data in the 'Society name' field. Perhaps it might be decided that the record number is an unnecessary feature of the printed list; printing instructions to the database package could include information about which fields to print and, in a further improvement, in which order to print them. The formatting allows the computer system to distinguish between one field and another and to give each field a distinctive treatment according to the instructions given by the user to the database package.

Quite sophisticated displays can be created, to provide a series of different 'views' of the same data. For example, entries in the printed version of the *British national bibliography* are all derived from a database where a full MARC record for every document recorded is held. Each record consists of many fields but only a small selection is used to create the printed entry. The printing instructions also include information about the typographic conventions to use: italics, bold type, capital letters and so on. Other fields in the record are used to create the entries in the alphabetic subject index and the author/title index. 'Views' can also be created for use on visual display units, using colour and other graphical means of emphasis. From one record can come, therefore, a 'cataloguer's view', which might comprise the whole of the MARC entry, a 'user's view', which might comprise a limited selection of fields to create a simplified catalogue entry, and a 'printed bibliography view'.

4.3 Database management systems

The term 'database management system' is fraught with problems. One difficulty is that, whilst it has a specific restricted meaning, it has been abused during the rapid emergence of microcomputers; any piece of software which stores information in records is in danger of being labelled a database management system whether it merits the label or not. A second problem is that some packages genuinely do not fit into one or other category of database software. In some cases this is because the software developers have recognized that different types of database software have useful features and have sought to incorporate those features into their software. In this section of the chapter a distinction is drawn between 'file managers', 'database management systems' and 'text retrieval systems'.

It is probably most useful to start with text retrieval systems since they are likely to be the most familiar to librarians. Consideration will then be given to database management systems, followed by file managers and finally personal bibliographic software.

Text retrieval software, as the name implies, was developed to cope with the storage and retrieval of textual matter. Thus it is useful to consider the characteristics of this type of data which necessitate special treatment. The first characteristic is that the data are largely alphabetic rather than numeric: examples are bibliographic records, a research scientist's laboratory notes and the full text of legal documents. Even where the data contain numbers, for example pagination data, they are usually treated as character strings. There is little need for the capability to perform computations on such data. Whilst it may be common in many libraries to create fairly small databases, the software emerged from an environment where it was necessary to cope with large amounts of data. Early examples of this type of software were created to handle upwards of 200,000 bibliographic records whilst, currently, the large bibliographic database, *Chemical abstracts*, contains of the order of ten million records. Not only was it expected that the database would contain a large number of records but that the records would be of considerable complexity and length. For example, a typical bibliographic record might contain 15 to 20 fields and some of those fields might contain a large amount of information. Typically there would be considerable overlap in the fields present in many different databases. It is common for the records to include an abstract of perhaps two hundred to three hundred words in an abstract field. A field for terms from the associated controlled vocabulary might contain 15 or more terms from the relevant thesaurus. The latter point illustrates a further feature of text retrieval systems, namely that the software must be able to deal with cases where any particular attribute has multiple values within a single record. A further, very obvious, need for this facility within a software package used for handling bibliographic records is the fact that so many items have multiple authorship. It can be seen from the discussion above that the length of a given field might vary considerably between records depending on, amongst other factors, whether or not the field contained multiple values.

A further feature of text databases is the complexity of the search features which are required. Whilst there will be some data which are used only for display and are not to be treated as searchable data (an example would be pagination data), most of the data need to be searchable. Not only must most words be searchable but they must be searchable in flexible and complex ways. The users of such databases typically wish to be able to retrieve records which contain various combinations of words. Sometimes it will be necessary to specify that the words sought appear in a particular proximity to each other, whilst on other occasions it will be necessary to retrieve those records which contain various combinations of search terms regardless of where in the record the terms occur. It may also be necessary to be able to specify that a particular term appears in a particular part of a record, say a named field. The latter would be useful, for example, to distinguish between books by Shakespeare and books about Shakespeare. It is apparent that this complexity of retrieval requirements cannot be met by ordering the database on the values of a single field or key field. Rather it is necessary to have a database organization which enables retrieval by a wide variety of search criteria. This is achieved by use of an inverted file structure.

Different software packages will use various methods of implementing the inverted file structure. From reading about software packages in publicity and other material, it is evident that there is no consistency in naming the various techniques and components used in creating inverted file structures. What follows is a hypothetical example which has been developed to illustrate the principle of the inverted file structure. It should not be thought that this example is based on any operational software, although the operation of all packages will bear a resemblance to this explanation.

A fictional, but not untypical, bibliographic record is presented in Figure 4.1. This is a somewhat simplified record; for example it does not contain fields indicating the language of the paper or any classification codes. Some of the details from the record are included in the sample of an inverted index which follows. In this hypothetical example of an inverted file structure the index can be thought of as consisting of three files, namely a 'print file', an 'index file' and a 'postings file'. The relationship between them is indicated in Figure 4.2.

Record no.:	02356
Authors:	Arkwright J.W.; Denmark P.S.
Title:	The history and development of the online information industry in the Republic of South Africa
Date:	1992
Details:	South African journal of information retrieval 87 (175) 227–252
Descriptors:	information industry, online searching
Identifiers:	Republic of South Africa, Southern Africa, hosts, database producers, 1970–1992
Abstract:	The paper provides the first comprehensive account of the development of the online information industry in South Africa. The reasons why some hosts have sought to market their products in this country are examined. An analysis of the most used search services and databases is presented. The importance of the development of the telecommunications infrastructure to the development of the industry is examined.

Fig. 4.1 An example of a bibliographic record (details fictitious)

Part of the Index file:

Postings	Terms	Postings file address
. . .	. . .	. . .
27	bibliographic	000236
135	database	000431
1	descriptors	000567
9	development	000634
8	hosts	000689
32	industry	000712
984	information	000923
36	market	001235
18	networks	001347
345	online	001423
78	telecommunications	001679
39	thesauri	000567
. . .	. . .	. . .

Part of the Postings file

Location	Term	Record numbers
. . .	. . .	. . .
000712	industry	00036,00184,02356 . . .
000923	information	00027,00197,02356 . . .
001423	online	00001,00256,02356 . . .
. . .	. . .	. . .

Part of the Print file

02355 . . .#
02356 Arkwright J.W.; Denmark P.S. The history and development of the online information industry in the Republic of South Africa 1992 South African journal of information retrieval 87 (175) 227–252 information industry, online searching Republic of South Africa, Southern Africa, hosts, database producers, 1970–1992 The paper provides the first comprehensive account of the development of the online information industry in South Africa. The reasons why some hosts have sought to market their products in this country are examined. An analysis of the most used search services and databases is presented. The importance of the development of the telecommunications infrastructure to the development of the industry is examined.#
02357 . . .#
02358 . . .#

Fig. 4.2 Hypothetical inverted file structure

The 'Print file' is that file which contains the information about each entity, in this case bibliographic information about documents. It is arranged by record number order, as is indicated in the diagram, so that the data represented by the record depicted in Figure 4.1 appear immediately after record number 02355 and before record number 02357. The 'Index file' is an alphabetic list of all those words which the program has been instructed to select for indexing. The information contained in the index file is the term, the number of times which it occurs in the database and a reference to a location, or address, in the postings file. Thus, in the case of the term 'information', the number of postings can be seen to be 984 and the address in the postings file can be seen to be 000923. The term 'market' has 36 postings and further information is stored at the address 001235 in the postings file. The 'Postings file' provides the vital link between the index file and the print file in that it contains a list of the accession numbers of records which contain that term. So, the term 'information' appears in record numbers 00027, 00197 and 02356 amongst others. The term 'online' appears in records 00001, 00256, 02356 and others.

When a searcher searches the database for the presence of a particular term, the software checks first against the index file. If the term is not present then a message to this effect will be displayed to the searcher. If the term is present then the response to the searcher will indicate the number of postings, that is the number of occurrences of the term sought. In a part of the memory of the computer set aside for temporary use by the database software, the software will retain a note of the address in the postings file for the term sought. If the searcher then instructs the software to print the items which match the search criteria (that is, those containing this particular term), the software simply notes the accession numbers at the relevant address in the postings file, uses these as a link to the location of the desired records in the print file, and displays the records in the manner requested.

The function of the postings file becomes more obvious in those cases where the searcher requires that the search is for those items which contain more than one designated term. If the searcher is seeking documents containing both the term 'industry' and the term 'information' (that is, a search involving the use of Boolean AND), then the software will check in the appropriate locations in the index file for the two terms and display the number of postings associated with each term. It will then employ a matching algorithm (a routine) which will note only those accession numbers which appear in the lists at both the addresses in the postings file. In the example given, the algorithm will detect that record number 02356 falls into this category. Such record numbers will be noted in the temporary work space and the total number of records will be displayed to the user as the number of items containing both the terms sought. A similar process occurs when the searcher specifies that the terms are linked by Boolean OR (that is, either one or both terms are present) or Boolean NOT (that is, the searcher requires those items which contain the first term but not the second term). The software will use a different algorithm for each type of search strategy.

Whilst the above explanation is accurate, it is also incomplete in a number of ways. In the first place it should be remembered that most text retrieval software will permit the user to define a list of stopwords, that is words which will not appear in the index file. These will usually be commonly occurring function words such as 'the', 'in', 'of', 'an' and so on, but they may also be words which appear with such frequency in a particular database that they are not useful search terms. The term 'laboratory' might not be thought to be a very discriminating term if used in a search on a database recording chemical techniques, for example. Furthermore, it should be noted that the previous paragraph referred continually to 'term' without indicating that a search term may be a single word or a phrase. One of the decisions which the software will enable the database designer to make is how specific fields are parsed for the creation of the entries in the index file. The most obvious option is for each word to be treated as a single word, but there will be cases where it is more appropriate to treat a phrase as the unit which is indexed and is, therefore, searchable. In a bibliographic database, the field containing the name of a journal would be a good example of a field which is best indexed as a phrase. A field containing terms taken from a thesaurus would be an obvious example of a field which may be best treated by ensuring that each word in a search term is indexed as well as each term being treated as a phrase; thus, for example, the term 'library security systems' could be indexed as the separate words 'library', 'security' and 'systems', and also as the complete phrase. Whilst these three options are the most obvious, the more sophisticated text retrieval packages may well offer further options.

Amongst the search features available in most text retrieval packages is the ability to specify the position of a word in a record. For example it may be important to specify that only those records in which the term appears in a selected field are retrieved. This may be necessary to ensure that only those items written by an author named 'London' are retrieved, and not all those items which are either published in London or about London. In a similar way, it is useful to be able to distinguish between 'penguin' as a subject and as the name of a publisher!

In addition it is frequently important to be able to specify the relative position of words in the retrieved records as a means of improving the relevance of the search. A geographer would obviously need to be able to distinguish items about the concept 'water table' from those about 'table water' and there is a considerable difference between the concepts of 'state police' and 'police state', to give only two very obvious examples. The reality, then, is that the postings file is rather more sophisticated that had been indicated in the earlier example. Not only does it contain information about the occurrence of a term within a record but it also contains information about where within the record the term appears. One method of achieving this is to record with the record number the field and the position within the field of each particular term. There are a variety of ways in which this can be achieved but the example indicated in Figure 4.3 is based upon the method used by the software BRS/Search, which is widely used, both by libraries and by commercial database search services. In this example only information for the record used in Figure 4.1 is presented. It can be seen that the postings file lists not only the record number but also the field within which the term occurs. In addition, the exact position within the field is indicated by pointing to the sentence within the field and finally the word within the sentence. Variants on this method may record the position of the term within the entire record or the field and then the position within the field. An alternative approach is to have a series of separate inverted indexes, the appropriate one of which is searched, depending on the request put to the system by the searcher.

In an effort to improve the ability to match enquiries from users, several packages have developed other stratagems. A popular, and useful, feature is that of phonetic matching, where words which sound alike will automatically be included in the retrieved set even though their spelling may differ. This is often useful in retrieving names of people; thus a search on the surname 'Clark' could also

Term number	Record number	Field number	Sentence number	Word
africa	02356	3	1	15
comprehensive	02356	8	1	6
databases	02356	8	3	10
development	02356	3	1	4
history	02356	3	1	2
hosts	02356	8	2	5
industry	02356	3	1	9
information	02356	3	1	8
online	02356	3	1	7
republic	02356	3	1	12
south	02356	3	1	14

Fig. 4.3 Sample from inverted file demonstrating one method of storing word positional information

retrieve 'Clarke', 'Clerk' and 'Klerk' if entries containing these names were included in the database.

4.4 Personal reference management software

In recent years a new variety of database software has appeared which can, most conveniently, be referred to as 'personal reference management' software. This software has been designed for use by academics and possibly by authors. The software is designed on the assumption that the data to be stored will be bibliographic and that the software must be simple to use. Thus it is usual for the package to come with a number of record structures already created for bibliographic data of different types. In addition there is usually some facility to create one's own record structure if required. Typically those available might include structures for making records about periodical articles, books, edited books, contributions to books, reports, patents and newspaper articles, and for less used materials, such as maps or computer programs. It is possible to store data for a variety of types of document within a single database. If the records are to be input from the keyboard, data input is usually aided by the offering of an easy to understand template on the screen. Whilst there are different structures to enable the storage of records for different types of bibliographic item, all the structures include fields for keywords, abstracts and notes. The latter feature is to permit a variety of comments such as locations and personal views on document content to be recorded. The search facilities offered by such packages are very variable. Some of them provide retrieval facilities comparable with those offered by a good text retrieval package. Others offer much more restricted retrieval facilities which may be little more than a search of a named field or fields, looking for a particular string of characters.

The novel feature of these packages is that they aid the process of constructing a bibliography for the end of a journal paper or the chapters of a book. It is possible to take references from the database, format these according to a designated bibliographic citation standard, and produce the bibliography and possibly the in-text citation according to an approved style. Typically the packages are sold with formats for a number of common citation styles, such as the Chicago system, the numeric system or the system adopted by some major journals such as *Nature* and *Science.* In addition, there is the facility to develop further citation styles to meet the requirements of journals for which the author writes regularly and which use their own citation style.

Many of the packages provide some facility for importing data from external sources and reformatting those data for incorporation into a local database. Sometimes some of these additional facilities for data importing are available by purchasing additional software. This software provides for the incorporation of data which have been acquired from a range of remote search services such as Dialog and CD-ROM producers such as Silver Platter. Together with any related packages, these personal reference management software packages offer considerable help to academic authors in the management of their reference collections and their writing. It might be more reasonable to consider them as productivity tools for academics.

Whilst these packages have been designed essentially for authors, the fact that they are designed for use with bibliographic data make them products of interest to librarians and information specialists. The ability to store a variety of bibliographic data structures in a single database and the fact that data inputting is aided by the field labels make them possible choices as the tool for creating a number of in-house databases. Furthermore, the fact that these packages often contain modules which aid the importing of data from other sources, such as CD-ROM or remote search services, makes the use of such packages advantageous as far as the process of database building is concerned. In an era where income generation is so important to many libraries, and the need to provide services to users is paramount, the availability of a database product which links readily with word processing software offers a wide variety of opportunities for the re-packaging of information.

4.5 Other search mechanisms

The standard text retrieval software has not been without its critics and researchers have sought to develop alternative approaches to text retrieval. Since those alternatives are now appearing in the market-place it is important to give some, albeit brief, consideration to such approaches. The approach adopted by most designers of text retrieval software has been to force it to partition the database into two sections when carrying out a search, namely one consisting of records which match the search criteria and another consisting of those which do not. The assumption behind this stratagem is that those which match the criteria are relevant to the searcher. There is no recognition in this approach that some records will be more relevant than others and that the most helpful response to a particular query would be to present the output to the searcher in decreasing order of similarity to the question posed. A further problem is that the searcher has no control over the size of the retrieved set and may need to learn various search tactics to manipulate the size of the retrieved set until it becomes acceptable. To achieve this the searcher needs to become familiar with the notions of Boolean logic and, in all probability, the command language associated with a particular piece of text retrieval software.

Information retrieval researchers have been concerned with developing approaches to retrieval which overcome these problems. A simple approach has been based on the notion that it is likely that documents containing *all* terms in a search statement, regardless of their Boolean relationships, are more likely to be relevant to a query than those documents containing only some terms. This approach is variously known as coordination level, or 'quorum function', searching. In this approach the user is presented, first, with those references which contain all the terms. These are followed by those items containing all but one of the terms and then by those items containing all but two of the terms and so on. Thus, some rough ranking is achieved by presenting the output to the user as a series of levels. An attempt can be made to provide some ranking within the various levels by utilizing the assumption that the term with the most postings is the worst discriminator and hence should be removed first. More sophisticated attempts have used methods of weighting both search terms and index terms and have made use of a variety of mechanisms for computing the similarity between the two. Some current research is seeking to produce ranked output on the basis of the proximity of words in records. The use of the technique of relevance feedback has shown some promise in recent years. This involves the development of a mechanism to build on responses of searchers about either retrieved items or features of those items which are deemed to be helpful or useful. Ellis has discussed this topic in greater detail.[1]

4.6 File managers

Generally speaking, file managers offer a much more restricted set of options to the database designer than do either text retrieval software or database management system software. There may well be a trade-off between sophisticated facilities and ease of use, in that use of a file manager may consist simply of selecting options from a menu or form-filling; another approach is to aid the user through the use of a graphical interface. Such packages limit use to a single file and the restrictions imposed on that file will be more severe than the limitations imposed by the more complex software types. For example, there may be more severe restrictions on the number of fields which can be placed in a record and the upper limit on both maximum record and field length may be quite small. In some of the simpler and cheaper versions, it may be possible only to index and, therefore, to search on the contents of a single field unless one is prepared for the use of string searching (that is, searching sequentially through the records looking for occurrences of a particular string of characters). There are unlikely to be any data validation facilities and the report generation functions, if there are any at all, will be considerably more restricted than in the other database software types. Nevertheless, it is quite plausible that the features offered by such software will be adequate for a particular task; after all there is little sense in purchasing a Rolls Royce if your only use for it is to go to the local shop and that task can be accomplished just as readily by purchasing a Mini. One of the better file handlers, and one that is so sophisticated that many may argue that it is in fact a text retrieval product, is Cardbox Plus, which is readily available in the United Kingdom. It is in regular use in many libraries for creating and using a variety of in-house databases.

4.7 Database management systems

Database management systems (DBMS) have their origins in commercial data processing and, whilst the first database packages appeared on mainframe computers, there are now a considerable number of widely available microcomputer-based packages which can fairly be called database management systems rather than file managers. The most widely known example is the dBase series of packages, but other well-known products include Superbase, Foxbase and Paradox. In the early days of commercial data processing, a typical organization would have had several related applications, all of which were in essence separate file processing operations with separate files and separate programs to manipulate the data in the way which was required by a given department. Thus it might be the case that the sales department and the accounts department were operating separate systems which were not compatible with each other. A library provides a good example of the procedures and the related problems, though once again it should be stressed that the example is a fictional one invented for the purposes of illustration rather than being based on any particular system.

Early examples of library automation might have included a catalogue file, a circulation file, an on-order file and a borrowers file, amongst others. Each of these would be processed by a suite of programs but, in all probability, the various automation functions would have been independent of each other. It should be self-evident that there would have been some overlap in the data elements necessary for each of these functions. For example, the acquisitions, circulation and cataloguing functions all require some information about particular books. However, each application also requires some information which is unique to itself. This approach of using separate files has obvious disadvantages, the most common of which are data redundancy and the opportunity for creating data errors. By 'data redundancy' is meant the fact that the same data are entered into a number of different files which are used for different purposes. Thus, basic bibliographic details might need to be generated several times for the various functions. If this has to be achieved by keyboarding then the opportunities for making errors and inconsistencies in the data are obvious. The 'database approach' stores a series of related files in a database in a structured way. Whilst in the earlier development of database systems there were numerous approaches such as network and hierarchy, it has become the case in recent years that the DBMS approach is almost synonymous with the development of a relational technique.

In a relational DBMS the data are stored as a series of tables which have been constructed according to well-defined rules. The software then provides the facilities for the data to be retrieved from the different tables and combined to meet the needs of a particular enquiry. In a hypothetical library automation system, the database might consist of the following tables:

Documents table

Document number	Document author	Document title	Document publisher	Document description

Borrowers table

Borrower number	Borrower name	Borrower address

Loans table

Document number	Borrower number	Date due

Orders table

Order number	Document number	Supplier code	Date ordered	Date received

Suppliers table

Supplier code	Supplier name	Supplier address

Not only does a relational DBMS enable data to be stored in a series of tables, as in the example, but it also provides facilities for the querying of those tables. This is achieved using the three basic commands, 'SELECT', 'PROJECT' and 'JOIN'. Use of these commands enables the creation of temporary tables which contain the information needed to answer a particular query. One of the advantages of the relational approach is this flexibility of temporary table creation. The data elements can be related in any manner necessary to answer a question. In the older file-based approach the relationships between data elements were only present if they had been created in advance by the designer. Some examples will demonstrate the use of the three basic commands.

The command 'PROJECT' is the simplest place to start, since it is used to create new tables from existing tables by the omission of some of the data elements. The general form of the command is:

PROJECT (name of existing table) OVER (list of required fields, or columns) GIVING (new table)

For example, the instruction:

PROJECT (Orders) OVER (Order number, Document number, Date received) GIVING (On order)

would provide a listing of those books which had been ordered and received.

Whilst the command 'PROJECT' is used to omit columns from the table, the command 'SELECT' is used to omit those rows which do not meet the search criteria. These criteria can be expressed using the familiar Boolean operators of AND, OR and NOT. Thus the form of a command using this command is:

SELECT (name of existing table) WHERE (condition(s)) GIVING (new table)

An example would be:

SELECT (Loans) WHERE (Date due <= '22.07.92') GIVING (Overdue documents)

A list of those documents in the database written by the authors 'Smith' or 'Jones' would be presented in a table by the command:

SELECT (Documents) WHERE (Document author='SMITH' or Document author='JONES') GIVING (Temporary table)

Useful as these operations are, it can be seen that they operate only on existing tables which are manipulated to create new tables. The real power of the relational approach is given by the use of the command 'JOIN'. This enables new tables to be created by taking elements from more than one existing table and merging them into a new table. The form of the JOIN command is:

JOIN (table 1) AND (table 2) OVER (column) GIVING (new table)

Thus the command:

JOIN (Documents) AND (Loans) OVER (Document number) GIVING (Temporary table 1)

will create a temporary table with the following elements:

Document number	Document author	Document title	Document publisher
Document description	Borrower number	Date due	

The command 'PROJECT' could then be used on this table to remove the 'Document description' column, following which the command 'SELECT' could be used on temporary table 1 to produce an overdue list which included bibliographic details rather than just the document number. By analogy it should be apparent that further use of the same commands could be specified to replace the borrower number with details of borrower name and borrower address. The reader may like to try to create the appropriate tables to demonstrate this.

There are additional techniques for analysing the data into a series of tables such as this; the database software provides facilities for the interrogation of the data so that attribute values from different tables can be linked together to provide answers to specific queries. This is known as data normalization and follows a standard set of rules. A full explanation of them is beyond the scope of this book but a brief example may suffice to illustrate their use.

Consider the data which might be held in a simple loans control system. For every loan, the system might record the following attributes:

Borrower number	Borrower name	Borrower address	Document number	Date due

It is clear that, in some cases, some of the information may be duplicated. For example, if the same borrower decides to take out two documents at the same time, the information about borrower number, name and address will be duplicated in the file. This is clearly a waste of space and, in the case of a large loans file, this waste might be quite large, leading to inefficient use of computer memory and increased processing times. In addition, if the address of the borrower should change whilst documents are still on loan, it would be desirable to update all loan records for this borrower number; although one could search through the file to find all occurrences of this number and make the necessary amendments, there is a distinct possibility of errors being made and occurrences being missed, quite apart from the tedium which might be associated with such a task. An improved design of system would enable one amendment to affect all occurrences of the number. Data normalization seeks to achieve this by recognizing that attributes fall into distinct categories and that a set of attributes representing an entity within those categories can be identified by some unique identifier. In the example given there is a 'Borrower' entity category with the attributes of 'Borrower number', 'Borrower name' and 'Borrower address'; within this category it is the attribute 'Borrower number' which is unique because other borrowers may be registered at the same address or may share the same name. There is also a 'Loans' entity category with the attributes 'Document number' and 'Date due'. For the purposes of a loans control system the two categories need to be linked. One approach might be to include the 'Document number' in the 'Borrower' entity category; this could prove troublesome, however, because several documents might be on loan to the same borrower and so the attribute 'Document number' would have to be repeated in this category. A more economical approach is to use the attribute 'Borrower number' as the link by including it in the 'Loan' entity. A document will never be on loan to more than one borrower at a time so this category need never contain more attributes than 'Document number', 'Borrower number' and 'Date due'. In this way, two tables can be defined for the loans control system:

Borrowers table: Borrower number, Borrower name, Borrower
address
Loans table: Document number, Borrower number, Date due

The process of normalization is, to some extent, instinctive for librarians and information workers who have absorbed the notions of facet analysis. The process of 'data analysis' can be conducted intuitively when dealing with sets of data with few entity types and a small range of attributes. However, for creating a system where there are many different types of attribute and entity the use of a systematic process is to be encouraged. Many texts describe the process which originated with the work, in 1970, of E. F. Codd on the development of a relational database model. This presented the process of normalization at three levels: first normal (1NF), second normal (2NF) and third normal (3NF) forms. The third level was later modified to become more robust and is now often known as the 'Boyce-Codd' normal (BCNF) form. Some data analysts have proposed a further succession of normal forms up to a sixth level. The interested reader may explore the rules and procedures described in many textbooks: Beynon-Davies[2] provides a good introduction to the process of normalization.

In addition to offering a means of storing data in a manner which minimizes data redundancy and provides extensive facilities for the retrieval of data from the database, DBMS also offer facilities for report generation and data recovery and data security. In addition most DBMS include a programming language. Whilst it is by no means essential to use the features offered by this programming language, its provision means that DBMS can be considered as development tools with which to produce a solution to a particular problem. An important, and recent, development in the application of DBMS packages across both mainframes and micros has been the development and implementation of a Standard Query Language, known as SQL, which is being implemented by most of the leading developers of DBMS software packages. As the name implies, this offers a standardized language with which to structure queries for the database. The intention is obviously to make life simpler for the user by ensuring that there is only one query language which needs to be learnt.

References

1   Ellis, D., *New horizons in information retrieval*, Library Association, 1990.
2   Beynon-Davies, Paul., *Information systems development*, Macmillan, 1989.

Chapter Five

Other organizing software

5.1 Introduction

Whilst spreadsheets and databases are generally seen as the most obvious candidate software types for data organization and management, there are several other types of software which may be appropriate in some circumstances. These include word processors, desk-top publishing systems, outliners, project managers, expert systems and hypermedia systems.

5.2 Word processors

Word processors might not seem to fall into the category of organizing software or, even, to be of use in data management. They are, however, a primary tool for organizing material because they enable text to be stored, copied, moved, adjusted and presented in a variety of formats. For many users the word processor is the main piece of software they will encounter and therefore careful choice is necessary to ensure it will meet their needs. Some word processors have been developed for specialized purposes, such as composing scientific texts where a large range of symbols are needed, or for use by children; in the latter text appears in large letters and a range of effects can be achieved by using simple commands. To provide a large range of word processing software is usually not necessary and may be unhelpful, especially if the users wish to swap files of word-processed text. Some word processors will accept files from other software and allow them to be 'translated' into the native format; another commonly available method is to allow the import and export of text in a standard format known as 'ASCII' (American Standard Code for Information Interchange). Although such techniques allow text to be exchanged, other features, such as underlining of text and use of special characters, may be lost in the conversion process and have to be re-inserted by editing the text. The process of exchanging text in this way can become very tiresome. The ideal circumstance is for everyone in an organization to be using copies of the same word processing program on the same type of microcomputer.

All word processors offer a common, basic, set of features enabling the user to adjust the format of the text through setting margin sizes, page length and line spacing. Type size can be varied and enhancements – such as underlining, use of bold characters, superscripts and subscripts – can be incorporated. The user can move the current typing point, indicated by a cursor, around the document in small steps such as a character or line at a time, or in larger blocks such as moving forward or backward by several pages. All word processors provide facilities for storing, retrieving and printing text and usually allow text from files on the same machine to be imported to the current file. It is also possible to move blocks of text, delete and re-arrange text, very easily.

It is sometimes said that one's first use of a word processor sets the standard by which all others will be judged. It is certainly true that the main source of comparison tends to be the methods by which the commands are given to the word processing program. Some programs require the user to type in a 'command line', often involving use of one or more special keys in association with the character keys. A typical sequence to underline a word might be to press the key marked 'CONTROL' and, at the same time, the 'U' key to turn the underlining on, type the word and then press 'CONTROL' again and and the 'U' key to turn the underlining off. Such procedures will take some time to become familiar but they have the advantage of being quick to use, once learnt. On the other hand, they may not be very easy to remember and the keystrokes for the little-used features, in particular, may be so unmemorable as to require several minutes with the user manual to discover. If command lines are used then one should look for a clear mnemonic structure. Some programs offer screen displays and 'help' pages which serve to remind the user of what commands and options can be selected. In the better programs such displays are 'context-sensitive': the display offers advice and reminders appropriate to the conditions. Other techniques used to facilitate the use of features include 'pop-up' and 'drop-down' menus from which the desired feature can be selected by moving a cursor or mouse pointer. The new user may find this approach much simpler and it can help less confident users to acquire word processing skills quickly.

Features additional to the basics are what sell word processors. The range is very wide but there are some commonly occurring items which it is worth considering. If documents with complex layouts and use of several sizes and shapes of type are planned, then a word-processor program offering 'wysiwyg' – 'what you see is what you get' – can be invaluable. This feature means that text will appear on the screen exactly as it will be printed, assuming, that is, that the printer attached to the microcomputer is capable of printing the range of characters and layouts used. 'Wysiwyg' allows the user to check that the appearance is exactly as required but it is a feature usually only found in the more powerful and expensive software. A partial substitute is a 'preview' feature allowing the user to see a much reduced page image of the text, which allows one to check layout but not the detail of the characters to be printed.

The range of characters available may be very important, especially if documents in languages other than English are to be prepared. A full range of accents, diacritics, punctuation and currency symbols, together with other specialized symbols may be needed; some texts in English may require special symbols to represent, for example, mathematical or logical constructs. Setting aside the specialized word processors, some of the general word processors offer a rich variety which should satisfy the needs of most writers. LocoScript PC is notable in this respect in that it supports the use of Cyrillic, modern Greek and ancient Greek alphabets (including a full range of breathing marks) and can, through the use of an additional program, support Arabic and Hebrew scripts. In addition, it is possible to design special characters to suit the needs of the user through a 'customization' program. Another program which offers a good range of symbols for languages and scientific word processing is Vuwriter. With any word processing program it is important to check that the printer attached to the system can be configured to print the range of characters available, however.

Text manipulation is at the heart of word processing. Rarely is one satisfied with the text just written, and alterations, re-arrangement and substitution are common functions which a good word processing program should provide and should make easy. 'Cut and paste' is the main facility; this allows the user to mark a block of text, copy it into a temporary store called a 'paste buffer' and then allow it to be inserted at the appropriate part of the same, or another, document. This facility can also be used to remove, or 'cut', an unwanted block of text. It is very useful to have several paste buffers available, especially if a complex document is being amended. An extension of this idea is the ability to store phrases ('Yours faithfully' or the name of an organization, for example) in special 'glossary' buffers so that they can be inserted as needed by using the 'paste' facility. 'Search and replace' offers a feature which will allow the user to define a word or phrase which should be substituted for another throughout a document and will then make these adjustments in the text, either automatically or by drawing the attention of the user to every occurrence.

It is also useful to be able to copy sections of text between documents so that a phrase from one can be used in another context. A feature which aids this type of text manipulation is the ability to display portions of more than one document on the screen at the same time. This 'windowing' technique usually allows the user to position the windows and adjust their relative sizes to suit and also to select the window within which the current range of actions will take place. Thus, for example, when copying text from one document to another it would be desirable to display the appropriate portions of both documents side by side, then select the window displaying the document from which to copy, mark the block and copy it to a paste buffer, select the window displaying the other document and then position the cursor within the window at the point where the block of text is to be added, completing the transfer by selecting the command 'paste'.

It is often helpful to be able to store an often used key sequence, or even a set of commands which are commonly used together, in the form of a 'macro'. These are small program segments written by the user and invoked by typing a key sequence selected by the user. The technique can be a boon if document preparation involves a set of frequently repeated actions. For example, quotations in a text may be shown in a special layout using indentation, a smaller type size than the main text and italics may be used; selecting these and adjusting the layout can take a lot of time and may be prone to error. Storing the key sequence necessary to select these options and the sequence to restore the layout of the main text as macros will greatly assist the user. A useful extension of this is the ability to invoke a 'looping' function which will allow the macro to be repeated a set number of times or until a condition, specified by the user, has been satisfied. This is especially useful if it is necessary to draw together a document from a sequence of sections of other documents held as separate files on the microcomputer.

The most erudite user will occasionally make errors when typing. A spelling checker is of help in detecting and correcting such 'typos' and will also assist those whose memory for spelling is not good. The checker is usually run as a separate activity after a document has been prepared, though there are a few which run alongside the main word-processing program and signal if a word has been entered which is not in the dictionary held by the checker. A well-conceived program will mark the offending word and offer the user a suggested substitute, but will also offer access to the dictionary so that other substitutes could be selected, and an opportunity to edit the word in error, to mark it as correct or to add it to an additional dictionary, called the 'user dictionary'. Spelling checkers often allow access to look up single words in the course of writing and allow checking of parts of documents as well as the complete text.

It is important to check that the dictionary of the spelling checker is both large enough and suitable for the language of composition. In particular it is important to distinguish between versions suitable for English and American English. It is usually possible to add words to a 'user dictionary', thus accommodating specialized terms and abbreviations. It can be irritating to find that the singular form of a word is in the main dictionary and the plural is missing and has to be added to the user dictionary. Some spelling checkers allow the creation of several user dictionaries so that several separate lists of specialized words can be maintained. It is rarely possible for the user to adjust the contents of the main dictionary; this lack can be a nuisance, especially if an organization has standardized on, say, 'ize' rather than 'ise' word forms and the spelling checker includes words with both forms. This would hinder one in using the spelling checker to ensure the standard is maintained. Spelling checkers for languages other than English are becoming more readily available and some are appearing with separate dictionaries dedicated to specialized subject areas. The specialized dictionary will contain common words as well as a full range of the technical vocabulary and jargon likely to be used in preparing documents discussing the specialized subject.

81

A thesaurus is often provided alongside the spelling checker so that it is possible to search for, and select, associated words, such as synonyms and antonyms. Some provide assistance to crossword solvers in the form of an anagram generator; conscience will dictate whether this feature is advertised in the library.

Another aid to composition is a 'grammar checker' which is, at present, bought as a separate program and run, like the spelling checker, after writing is completed. Grammar checkers are at an early stage of development and are not very sophisticated, partly because the grammatical construction of a language is complex and especially so if the language is English. They are useful, however, for simpler checks such as the accidental repetition of words, use of clichés and the presence of double negatives. The range of features and sophistication is likely to improve as developers of word processing software compete.

Many writers appreciate a word-count feature. This is of great assistance for those who have to meet a limit, especially if the word-count is readily apparent on screen as text input proceeds. Some programs offer word-count only at the time the text is stored or as a by-product of the operation of the spelling checker. Before relying on the word-count it is worth investigating how it deals with words including hyphens, punctuation symbols (such as apostrophes) and numbers. Some programs will ignore words containing such features, thus reducing the accuracy of the count.

Footnotes are often required in academic texts or in formal reports. The numbering and placement of these can be a tiresome job, especially if the text is changed several times and the footnote positions and numbering need to be adjusted. Some programs now include automatic numbering which will adjust as footnotes are removed or additional footnotes are added earlier in the sequence.

Another task which may be assisted is the creation of an index from the finished text. The usual procedure is for the indexer to go through the text and mark with a special symbol words or phrases to be included in the index. The program will store these marked sections together with the relevant page number, assemble and sort them into whatever order is chosen and then display them for editing. Some programs allow the indexer to specify inverted phrases and automatic generation of cross-references. At this stage of development many are quite difficult to use, however, and the quality of the finished index will depend more on the skill of the indexer in editing than in the intrinsic power of the program in generating the index.

'Mailmergers' are included with some word processing programs. They allow the user to create a standard document, such as a letter, which is going to be sent to several people and will contain some information common to all but also some information, such as names and addresses, specific to the recipient. The mailmerge feature facilitates this by allowing the user to substitute special codes into a special form of the document, called a template; the codes are linked to a file containing the information specific to the recipient and are used by the program to retrieve the needed items, recipient by recipient, and substitute them for the codes in the template. Although the sole use of mailmergers might seem to be for producing 'form' letters, the use can be extended to other tasks where, for example, there is a need to send material to personnel or library members.

Several word processing programs include additional devices to assist in the preparation of text. An on-screen, 'pop-up' calculator may be useful if financial or other reports containing figures are to be prepared. The calculator can be called when needed and will temporarily overlay part of the display on the screen. The image looks like a small pocket calculator, complete with a picture of a keypad and display. Numerals and functions are entered either by using the numeric keys on the keyboard of the computer or by using a mouse to select the 'buttons' on the keypad image. The calculator display shows the result of the calculation and this may be immediately inserted into the text of the document, if needed. An extension of this idea is the ability to import tables and other data from a spreadsheet directly without a lengthy conversion process. The most sophisticated manifestations of this allow 'dynamic' links which automatically change the appropriate figures in the document if the data in the spreadsheet are altered.

Another useful feature is a pop-up 'filer', which allows a small database to be built and used within the word processor. Several files can usually be maintained so that personnel details, lists of members of a library or information service or records of current events, for example, can be maintained and selected as appropriate. The details from each entry are displayed on a small card image and can be incorporated into the text of a document, as needed. The more sophisticated programs allow for sorting and indexing of the files in several different sequences, defined by the user, and provide fast means of searching the files. It is also possible to print out the contents of each file, change and delete items and incorporate entries into a mailmerge template.

Apart from using the word processing software as a substitute for a typewriter in preparing reports and other administrative material, there are many other ways in which its power can be used to assist in library or information service management. Preparing publicity material is an example; the range of type sizes and styles can, if used with discretion, enable attractive posters and notices to be prepared. If combined with the use of a photocopier which can enlarge the image, the result can be very satisfactory. Another possibility is the preparation of bibliographies and lists of additions to stock. If the names and addresses of people interested in particular subject areas are maintained on a pop-up 'filer' (and suitable steps are taken to comply with the requirements of the Data Protection Act in respect of the storage of personal details) then subject lists can be prepared and a form of current awareness service introduced. Some care must be taken in the use of such filers: they are not as flexible or as able, usually, to store as much data as a database program. If the list of entries is more than about two hundred entries, and several different fields may be used to retrieve data, the use of a database program may be more efficient. Some word processing programs will allow data held on such database programs to be imported into documents.

Another use of word processing programs is to 'post-process' the results of an online search. Some communication programs, used to set up the communication link with an online service, will allow the results of the search to be recorded in a file which, after the search has ended, can be edited using a word-processing program to remove, for example, the commands which have been used to carry out the research. Some attempt might also be made to improve the appearance of the search results by, for example, underlining titles of documents or using bold characters. Records of dubious relevance might be deleted from the results and introductory material added, indicating, for example, whom to contact for further information. Specialized software to carry out such post-processing has also become available (Refwriter, for example) and this enables other tasks, such as sorting of results, to be carried out very easily.

Many libraries and information services need a range of forms for various administrative functions. The cost of printing these can be considerable, especially if the number required is not large. A more economic option is to design and store the form, using a word processing program, as a template. It is easy to use the program to copy the form and then also use it to enter and edit details on the form. Changes to the template can easily be made and if multiple copies are needed, the template can be printed out and photocopied.

Templates can also be used to set up standard letters. Suppose, for example, the hours of opening are to be changed; one could include a paragraph about this as part of a letter template, thus ensuring that it appears on every letter sent out in which it is appropriate.

The word processing program is a ubiquitous piece of software and new versions are frequently released with additional features. Whilst the temptation may be to acquire the program which includes the most advanced features, it must be remembered that the quest for sophistication includes its own penalty: the time that must be invested in acquiring the knowledge to 'drive' the program. If one's needs are fairly simple, then a program offering a complex range of features may be irritating and lead to frustration.

5.3 Desk-top publishing

An extension of word processing is text presentation in a 'camera-ready' form, so that it can be printed without the additional expense of typesetting. The process involves the use of a special 'desk-top publishing' (dtp) program which allows text, previously prepared in a word processor, to be manipulated and laid out in the form of book pages, newspaper columns, leaflets and other forms. Because the images on the screen are 'bit mapped' it is possible to manipulate the characters in the text and display them in a variety of different typefaces, combine them with other bit-mapped images, such as graphics and photographs which have been converted using a scanner, and then move them around, allowing text to flow around pictures and diagrams, and so on. The range of effects is very wide and will match the ingenuity of most users. The range may be so wide, in fact, that early attempts take on the bizarre form of a poster advertising a circus, with lurid colours, use of several typefaces in different sizes, and a dazzling combination of text and graphics. Although this may satisfy the desire of the tyro user to display mastery over the program, it presents an uncomfortable appearance to the reader.

Used with discretion and an eye to good design, the desk-top publishing program can be an excellent way of improving the appearance of publications from the library or information service. To make the fullest use of these programs a laser printer is essential, although some can be configured to produce output of a lower quality on ink-jet and 24-pin dot-matrix printers. It is essential, when purchasing a desk-top publishing program, to check that it will support the printer attached to the microcomputer. Fortunately, most programs communicate with the printer through a standard 'page description language' (PostScript is a common example) which is built into a small additional computer in the printer. This allows the program to support a wide range of printers.

Desk-top publishing programs can also be useful for producing graphics, charts and tables which can then be output on a laser printer in the form of transparencies ('foils') for overhead projectors. Once again the virtues of simplicity are worth remembering if a cluttered image is to be avoided. Specialist, and expensive, 'presentation graphics' software is available for those with a need to produce slides of a very high quality, incorporating complicated graphics, a wide range of colours and typefaces.

Anyone contemplating using a desk-top publishing program should be prepared to invest several days in becoming familiar with the software. To achieve good results careful thought and practice are needed and it is worth bearing in mind that well-designed output from a word processing program may be just as acceptable and somewhat simpler to produce.

5.4 Outliners

An 'outliner', sometimes called an 'ideas processor', is either a vital tool for a writer or an irritating, costly and inadequate substitute for pencil and paper. The principle is simple: in writing a long or short document a primary stage is often to list the topics to be included and then try to shuffle them about until a coherent order is achieved. These topics often form an hierarchy of headings and sub-headings with, perhaps, a few words of explanation. A frequent need is to be able to swap headings around and to alter their relative placement in the hierarchy. The outliner program provides this facility and will usually allow the writing plan to be exported to a word processor or printed. Some word processing programs include an outliner and, in this case, the transfer is simple and quick. In other cases the file containing the plan may have to be exported in an ASCII format and then read into the word processing program and converted into its native format.

An extension of this idea, sometimes provided if the outliner is integrated with a word processing program, is a 'notepad' which can be summoned to 'pop-up' and overlay the text on screen; this provides a handy place for the ideas which occur during writing and ensures that they are not as easily lost as scraps of paper.

5.5 Project managers

In running any project, resources need to be specified and acquired and their use coordinated. Project management tools aim to help with these requirements by providing a structured means of storing a set of resource requirements; scheduling and sequencing events in the life of the project in such a way that the resource requirements can be used efficiently; and monitoring progress on achievement of objectives, drawing attention to events which are not proceeding according to the plan.

Software for project management tends to be quite expensive and it takes quite a long time to use it properly. Also, some knowledge of the underlying theory behind the techniques used is necessary if the results are to be interpreted with due care. The packages are not, then, for the gifted amateur and may not be necessary for the library or information service manager with only a small project to control. Pencil and paper techniques may be quite sufficient in these circumstances. If, however, the project requires the careful sequencing of the use of a lot of resources, if the timetabling and completion date is critical or if there are many different sequences in which it might be completed, then using a project management software package may yield a more successful plan.

Three main 'tools' are provided by most packages: Gantt charts, network tools – principally Critical Path Analysis (CPA) or Programme Evaluation Review Technique (PERT) – and Work Breakdown Structures. Gantt charts are drawn as bar charts showing the beginning, end and duration of an activity in relation to a time line. As a task proceeds, progress is shown by gradually filling in the bar in relation to the time line. Thus it is possible to inspect the chart at any time and see which tasks started on time and have been finished, which have been delayed or have been started ahead of time, and which are falling behind the schedule. The software facilitates the drawing of the chart by prompting the user to key in a list of tasks and planned art and finish dates. The initial chart is then produced and may be printed for permanent display or stored. The stored chart may be updated as the project proceeds by inputting the proportion completed by the current date. A revised chart can then be output which includes a partial filling-in of the task bars to represent progress.

Network tools require similar information to Gantt charts, with additional information about the sequence in which tasks can be done and the duration of each task. The software package will then calculate and display a network representing the set of activities and identifying the critical sequence which defines the minimum time necessary to complete the project. It is possible to identify from the chart free, or 'float', time which could be re-allocated to other tasks to assist their early completion or to redress any delay. The results may be printed out or stored for later use and amendment. The particular value of using software for this type of network creation is the ability to re-run the problem using a different set of assumptions and see what effect this might have on the network and overall completion times.

Work Breakdown Structures are best thought of as being similar to organization charts showing hierarchies of responsibility and groupings of tasks. The software provides ready-made symbols and line-drawing tools to produce charts.

A useful feature to look for in the printing routines is the ability to be able to rotate the printout through 90 degrees so that wide charts can be printed sideways on to whatever size of paper is being used in the printer.

5.6 Expert systems
Expert systems have emerged as a tangible result of research in artificial intelligence. This is not the place to become involved in a detailed discussion of artificial intelligence and its relevance to library and information work. Nevertheless it is important to avoid being over-awed by the terms 'artificial intelligence' and 'expert systems', a terminology which all too readily leads one to think in terms of intelligent machines or learning machines or, even, some sort of mystical domination by computers. One practical result of research in artificial intelligence has been the emergence of a variety

of commercial software products known as 'expert system shells'. These packages enable the user, who need not be a programmer, to organize 'knowledge' in particular ways so that the output of the programs is not a set of bibliographic references or a list of potential sources of information; rather, it is guidance on how to act in a particular situation or, possibly, a diagnosis of a fault or problem which may lead to a recommended course of action.

The notion of a computer containing knowledge is worth some brief consideration since it is this which gives rise to the ideas of intelligent machines with all their threatening implications. It appears that the term 'knowledge' is used in a much more cavalier fashion by practitioners in artificial intelligence than by many other sections of the community. To some extent this can be justified by the fact that it is very difficult to define knowledge in any meaningful way. Perhaps you would like to try before you continue reading. Generally 'knowledge' is associated with 'understanding' on the part of human beings. Whether or not you wish to think in terms of machines understanding in any meaningful sense is almost a matter of definition and personal preference. Thus it could be that the material included in an expert system might be referred to as 'data' or 'information' or 'knowledge' by different people with different preferences. For example, in the second edition of the *Anglo American cataloguing rules* (AACR2) there are a number of rules about access points in catalogues. The simplest of these is for the case of an item with a single author: it states, 'enter a work by one author under the heading for that person'. This might be represented in an expert system as:

IF a work is the responsibility of a single author THEN enter the work under the heading for that person.

Many expert systems consist of a series of such statements, as will be indicated later in this chapter. The reader may wish to consider whether such expressions are best considered to be 'data', 'information' or 'knowledge'. A pragmatic view is to suggest that it does not much matter how these statements are viewed; rather, the important matter is whether or not they can be used to produce useful systems.

The well-known examples of expert systems which are referred to frequently in the literature were designed for such tasks as medical diagnosis, geological ore prospecting, the interpretation of the outcome of analyses of chemical compounds and the configuring of computer systems. These are all highly skilled tasks which require considerable knowledge and are only performed by a human expert in the particular field. It is because these systems seek to mimic the performance of human experts that they are known as expert systems. Since they perform tasks which in a human being would be deemed to be the province of an intelligent and highly knowledgeable individual, it is all too easy for expert systems to be presented in a sensational manner. However, despite this origin in artificial intelligence research, and the sensationalist manner in which they are sometimes presented, expert systems are being increasingly used to organize and utilize knowledge in a number of everyday situations in industry and commerce. Examples of organizations using expert systems in their daily operations include Cardiff City Council, Eastern Electricity, General Accident Life and Shell International Petroleum.

Cardiff City Council has developed a prototype system for the valuation of council houses under the government's 'Right to buy' scheme. The council already maintains a database of all council house sale transactions. This is useful for future valuations if the information can be made available to valuers in a clear and consistent form. The expert system is able to combine information from this database together with information from a site inspection to offer a valuation. This use speeds up the process of valuation and thereby releases the valuers for more productive work. This increase in productivity typifies one of the commercial advantages of expert systems.

Eastern Electricity has developed a system which enables industrial sales engineers to answer the technical questions of potential customers without recourse either to bulky documentation or to the organization's technical experts. The system operates in the field of industrial drying systems for products such as metals, chemicals, food, paper, plastics and textiles. This system illustrates two important features of expert systems. The first is that they operate in restricted subject areas or 'domains', in the jargon, in much the same way as a human expert does. The second is that one of the beneficial features of expert systems is that they are making more widely available expertise which is already accessible within the organization. In this case that means that the technical knowledge of the expert in industrial drying systems is now distributed amongst all the sales engineers. The outcome is that the sales engineers can offer an improved service to potential clients whilst the expert in industrial drying systems can concentrate on the specialized aspects of the job without having to provide answers to technical questions from sales engineers.

General Accident Life has developed prototype applications in two areas. The first is in the processing of life underwriting and the second is in the shortlisting of candidates for job interviews. In the first case the information presented in a proposal document is matched against company policy and any problem cases are identified for action. In the second case, a similar matching procedure is adopted and the experience, qualifications, and so on, of candidates are matched against company expectations. The candidates can then be categorized as either 'interview', 'reject' or 'review'. In the expected manner of operation the applications of all candidates assigned to either of the two latter categories would be reviewed by an appropriate supervisor. It is reported that implementation of this system is saving the company more than £20,000 a year. In both of these cases a further feature of expert systems in operation is revealed: they offer a mechanism whereby expertise within a company can be moved further down the management chain. Thus, in both cases, the initial evaluation would be performed by a clerical assistant aided by the expert system and only cases in which there was some doubt or complication would be passed further up the organizational hierarchy.

Shell International Petroleum are utilizing expert systems in two areas of significant commercial importance. The first is to enable fire hazard analysis at liquid petroleum gas plants to be performed by non-expert staff. This, again, typifies the use of expert systems to make the expertise of a small number of domain experts available wherever it is needed within the company. The second enables the more effective management of the very expensive metal, silver, which is used in some chemical reactions. All these commercial applications have been developed using a microcomputer-based expert system shell which is readily available and relatively inexpensive.

These brief descriptions of a number of small-scale operational expert systems reveal a number of the features which are characteristic of expert systems. They operate in restricted domains. They make a scarce expertise more widely available within an organization, thus enabling a faster response to a situation and leaving the human expert free to concentrate on the more difficult problems. In many cases knowledge or expertise is moved down the organizational hierarchy, again with the result that the expert is left free to concentrate on more complex cases. An additional feature of expert systems which is worth noting is that they perform consistently: they do not suffer from illness or 'off' days, though their use can be prevented temporarily by equipment failure, of course. From a consideration of these characteristics it is relatively easy to conclude that expert systems can be successfully applied in situations where there is a clearly defined domain which is of a manageable size. There should be an obvious gain to the organization in a way which is measurable and, hence, identifiable. Greater profitability, reduced costs, increased productivity and improved safety are amongst the tangible benefits which an expert system should bring to an organization, if it is used in a suitable way.

In the field of library and information science there have been numerous experimental applications of expert systems techniques. Some have examined the feasibility of an expert cataloguing system which incorporates the AACR2 rules into either a catalogue advice-giving system or a cataloguing system. Others have investigated the use of an expert system as an aid to consistent classification. Attempts in this sphere have largely concentrated upon the presentation within an expert system of a classification scheme such as the *Dewey decimal classification* rather than making any attempt to mimic the process of classification, which would still be undertaken by the librarian. Further research has investigated the use of an expert system as an interface to remote search services such as Dialog. This work has resulted in the availability of one commercial product. These research efforts have all been relatively large-scale projects and, in the latter case, have involved significant programming effort using a variety of expert systems techniques. However, the benefits which are being experienced in industry and commerce are through the application of expert systems development packages (or shells) at a relatively low level within an organization where useful savings can be made or gains in productivity made by the application of a fairly simple system. It is likely that similar gains could be made in the library sector by the application of expert systems in areas such as book selection or the provision of information to library users. In the former case, a library's book selection policy could be incorporated within an expert system for utilization by a library assistant. It ought to be possible to categorize potential purchases as certainties for purchase, certainties not for purchase and uncertain items. Professional judgement could then be reserved for consideration of items in the final category. Similarly, much routine library advice and information could be incorporated into an expert system for use either by library users or library assistants in their dealings with the library's clientele. These would not be sophisticated systems but would cover simple applications such as library borrowing regulations, opening hours and, possibly, simple guidance on the contents of the collection.

The essential components of an expert system are a knowledge base in which knowledge about a particular domain is stored and an inference mechanism which enables conclusions to be drawn about a particular situation by comparison of the situation with the knowledge stored in the knowledge base. Expert system development tools, usually referred to as 'expert system shells', consist of an inference mechanism, or inference engine, and a knowledge structure, or knowledge structures, into which knowledge of the particular problem can be stored. In addition there will be an interface with the user and a variety of development tools to aid the system developer. They are referred to as 'expert system shells' because they can be seen, initially, as expert systems which lack domain-specific knowledge. The task of the system designer is to fill the shell with the knowledge peculiar to the domain.

The knowledge base can contain knowledge in a variety of different structures. By far the best known of these is a 'rule-based' or 'production rule' system. In these systems the knowledge is represented as a series of rules of the variety:

IF antecedent THEN action

Thus, a possible rule for an intelligent interface to a remote search service might be:

IF search retrieves too many items THEN
implement search-narrowing tactics

and one example of a search-narrowing tactic might be expressed as:

IF no narrower search terms are available AND IF
search output is still too large THEN consider
restricting output by language

In a manner such as this the tactics used by a skilled online searcher could be incorporated into a package which could be available as an easy-to-use intelligent interface for end-users.

The inference engine is the mechanism within an expert system which enables it to match the information collected about a current situation and match that against the knowledge in the knowledge base and thereby to offer advice, or draw conclusions about, a particular situation. The inference engine is usually referred to as being either 'forward-chaining' (i.e. data driven) or 'backward-chaining' (i.e. goal driven). In a goal-driven inference engine, the system starts with a particular goal or outcome and seeks to find evidence to support that goal. This approach is particularly suitable in circumstances where there are not many possible outcomes. For example, in a system which is intended to guide librarians in the correct application of the AACR2 rules, there is only one possible outcome or goal: namely, that the book is catalogued. The book is correctly catalogued if the relevant rules have been applied regarding the physical description of the book and the choice of heading(s). The system will operate by seeking evidence that all the appropriate rules have been applied and thus that the book has been correctly catalogued. In a forward-chaining mechanism the system starts by matching the information about a current situation with the antecedents in the rules in the knowledge base, and where a match occurs the rule operates, or 'fires', in the jargon. Forward-chaining is most useful in a situation where there are many possible outcomes. An example might be in the chemical analysis of an unknown compound; there could be many possible outcomes because the purpose of the analysis is to determine which of the several million known chemical compounds a particular sample is most likely to be.

It is reasonable to argue that a human expert operates by a mixture of both forward-chaining and backward-chaining reasoning procedures. As an example, consider a visit to a doctor. The initial questioning by the doctor will consist of some general questioning about the ailment which has caused the visit. After a short time this is likely to result in the doctor narrowing down the affliction to a small number of candidate ailments. At this stage the doctor will ask questions which are targeted towards gathering further evidence in favour of, or against, the complaint being one of the candidate ailments. The first part of the diagnosis is forward-chaining, moving forward from the data towards a solution, but the later questioning is an example of backward-chaining since the questioning is intended to find evidence in favour of, or against, a particular goal (in this case, diagnosis of a particular illness). The more sophisticated expert system shells provide both forward- and backward-chaining capabilities.

Expert systems operate by comparing information about a particular situation with the knowledge held in their knowledge bases. As a simplistic example, a knowledge base for forecasting the weather might contain a rule such as:

IF it is cloudy THEN it will rain

and the system might ask:

is it cloudy?

and if it receives the answer 'yes' then it would proffer the advice:

it will rain

Clearly a real system would contain many such rules. The outcome of one rule might well become the input for application of a further rule; thus complex sequences of rules can be built up to encompass the knowledge about a particular task or situation. It is likely that an expert system shell will provide a variety of mechanisms for collecting details of the current situation and matching that information against its knowledge base. The simplistic rule illustrated above also serves to introduce a further feature of many expert systems: a capability of dealing with uncertainty. Obviously it is not absolutely certain that it will rain when it is cloudy but this is a much more likely outcome than if the sky is bright blue. A variety of mechanisms have been utilized for dealing with uncertainty. Some are rather controversial but many appear to have the pragmatic benefit that they have operated successfully in at least one expert system. Further detail is beyond the scope of this book. The interested reader will be able to find a fuller explanation of expert systems in many textbooks on the subject, one of which has been written with information managers in mind.[1] Whilst sets of production rules are the best-known knowledge representation structure, there are other frequently used knowledge representation techniques, such as semantic networks and frames. In a semantic network a series of nodes are connected by links (some writers refer to them as 'arcs'). The nodes represent entities and the arcs indicate the relationship between those entities. A simple example is indicated in Figure 5.1. In this example, it can be seen that Peter is a lecturer who works at the University College of Wales (UCW), Aberystwyth, whilst his wife is a librarian in Oxford. Furthermore, it can be seen that neither of these facts is explicitly stated in the diagram; rather, they are inferred from the diagram. This is because the principle of inheritance applies: the network records that Peter works in the Department of Information and Library Studies (DILS). Since this department is based in an institution which, in itself, is based in Aberystwyth, Peter inherits the property of working in Aberystwyth. Semantic networks are not without problems; one is that some knowledge is not easily represented in this formalism. For example,

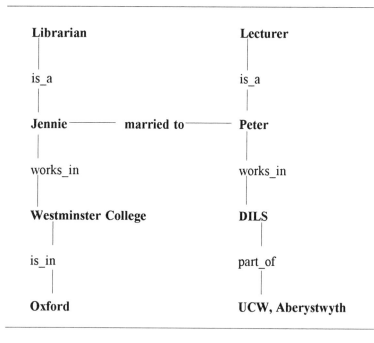

Fig. 5.1 Simple semantic network

statements such as 'most librarians are chartered', or 'many microcomputers have colour monitors', cannot be satisfactorily presented in semantic networks. Furthermore, the inference strategies necessary to utilize knowledge stored in this manner can be complex. Frames, or schemata, can be viewed as extensions of semantic networks. Again, they are data structures for storing knowledge about objects and well-defined events. The interested reader should seek further details from a basic text on expert systems or artificial intelligence.

In some complex knowledge-based systems, the knowledge may be split into several separate modules. An advantage of this approach can be that different modules may use different knowledge representation strategies. This has been done in the intelligent online search product TOMESEARCHER, which uses production rules, semantic networks and frames in different modules. In the case of this system the modules are utilized sequentially; however, in some systems which utilize a number of modules of knowledge (knowledge sources), a technique known as 'blackboard systems' is used. These knowledge sources may interact with a 'blackboard' which might contain information about the current state of the problem solution and can be used to pass information between the various knowledge sources. The analogy is taken from the use of a blackboard as a device for sending messages between a group of workers who seek to tackle a problem.

5.7 Hypermedia

Hypermedia has, in recent years, replaced expert systems as the computing technology which is generating most excitement. It is perhaps useful to start this discussion by making the distinction between 'hypertext', which contains text only, and 'hypermedia', which may consist of a mixture of text, graphics and images. Whilst the surge of interest in, and construction of, practical hypermedia systems is recent, the idea behind it is not new: it originates from about 1945. The hypermedia concept has its origins in the idea that people use libraries in a non-sequential way and that, indeed, they frequently use books or other documents in a non-sequential manner. It is argued that the reader seeks for information and follows up clues and leads in a complex pattern of movements until an information need is satisfied. In 1945 Vannevar Bush[2] propounded the notion that at some future date access to all the world's scientific literature would be available at the desk of working scientists. Furthermore, any such system would provide for the non-sequential movement through material which had been observed to be the normal human behaviour. He called this personal documentation system 'memex'. For many years this remained a theoretical possibility and, certainly, his technological speculations on how this might be achieved have not been accurate. However, recent developments in computer hardware and software have led to the development of software products which take us at least partway down the road to this, apparently utopian, system.

The key feature of hypermedia, as indicated in the preceding paragraph, is the notion of non-linearity of information selected and used by an enquirer. This non-linearity is achieved by having units of information which can be related through the means of associative links. The units of information may be blocks of text or they could be graphical, audio or video information. In the case of hypertext the blocks of information are solely textual. The links within a hypertext system may be one of two kinds, namely 'permanent' links, which are defined by the system builder, or 'temporary' links, which are created by the system user. Whilst this flexibility of navigation through a mass of information is clearly a revolutionary approach, it has the obvious corollary that there is a tendency for the user to become disorientated within the system. Attempts to overcome this disorientation are made through the use of graphical interfaces and various other devices.

Perhaps the best known of the available hypermedia systems is HyperCard, which is available for Apple Macintosh microcomputers. In HyperCard the unit of information is the card. Cards on related subjects are grouped in stacks which can be thought of as files. Usually a card contains only a screenful of information, although there is provision for more. Buttons (created on the screen as graphic images) enable the user to start a HyperCard function (creating a link to another card, for example) by selecting an appropriate button using a pointing device such as a mouse. The creator of a stack of cards can authorize access at a variety of different levels: that is to say, permitting access to a range of different facilities. The lowest-level access is usually the 'browsing' function, which only enables the user to browse through a stack of cards. The next level is 'typing', which permits the user the same facilities as browsing together with the facility to amend any fields which are not protected (or 'locked'). 'Painting' permits the same facilities as the two lower levels together with the ability to alter the screen appearance using a software package called MacPaint. 'Authoring' enables the user additionally to create new stacks of cards, link stacks and amend fields, buttons or cards. The highest level of access, 'scripting', adds the ability to create scripts and to use the programming language Hypertalk. Probably the best-known application of HyperCard is the Glasgow Online system which was devised in the Department of Information Science at the University of Strathclyde and initially tested by use at the Glasgow Garden Festival in 1988. This system provides a guide to Glasgow intended for use by residents, tourists and anyone else interested in the city. The system contains information about accommodation, shopping, places of interest, places of worship, local government, food and drink and many other features of the city. The various subject areas are represented graphically on the opening screen of the system and each of the graphic representations, such as 'places of worship', represents a stack of cards. Each of the stacks is organized into an hierarchic structure. The user can move up and down hierarchies or can follow predetermined routes or trails which have been built into the system and are non-hierarchical. Since the end-user has only 'browse'-level access, only connections which have been provided by the creators of the system can be followed. A similar HyperCard guide to a locality is Gateshead Hypertour Tourist Information System, which has been developed by Gateshead Libraries and Arts Department and is available for use at their location in the Gateshead Metro Centre, the largest indoor shopping centre in Europe.

The GUIDE system is a hypermedia package which runs on MS-DOS microcomputers, the Apple Macintosh or powerful workstations such as those produced by Sun Microsystems and DEC. GUIDE does not use the concept of cards; rather, it uses hierarchically structured text, known as Guidelines. Although the text is hierarchically structured, it appears to the user as a continuous sequence of text. Users can move through the text in a non-sequential manner using buttons which are embedded in the higher-level text. GUIDE has been used to produce a legal database, JUSTUS, containing information from primary and secondary legal sources ranging from dictionaries to cases. It has also been used to produce a library guide for use as part of a library induction programme at Bournemouth University.

From these examples it can be seen that hypermedia represents an important development in the storage of information, particularly in its simple retrieval and presentation to the user. Whilst there are obviously problems, in particular with seeking a way of preventing the user from getting lost in the system, it appears to be a technology which can be used for the presentation of information about a library to its users or for the development of a system which offers information about a locality. In some situations it may also be a technology which can be used successfully to present reference material to users.

References

1 Ford, N., *Expert systems and artificial intelligence: the information manager's guide*, Library Association, 1991.
2 Bush, V., 'As we may think', *Atlantic monthly*, **176** (1), 1945, 101–8.

Chapter Six

Starting the first data management project

6.1 Introduction

In the preceding chapters the general context in which a data management project is undertaken has been discussed and the various software options have been outlined. The purpose of this chapter is to offer advice on how to go about a project. It has been assumed that this guidance is being written for the complete beginner, but with the hope that there will be some points of value to more experienced users. The discussion begins with advice on how to proceed with a microcomputer-based data management project and continues with advice on the identification and subsequent evaluation of software.

6.2 Getting started

The first task in any data management project should be to develop a clear view of the objectives of the project. This requires careful thought and preparation with pen and paper. At all costs, it is important to avoid the temptation simply to work at the keyboard without a clear outcome in mind. It is likely that the first task should be the preparation of a written specification of the task to be achieved. The specification should include not only a clear statement of the objectives of the project but also a clear recognition of the constraints of time and money under which the project is operating. It is important to be realistic in your objectives. The specification should be written in non-technical language and should concentrate on the objectives of the project and not on the implementation of the project. Do not be deterred by the fear that your specification will change as the project proceeds; this is almost certain to be the case and it should be viewed as part of the development process.

If you are completely new to the use of microcomputers then your next step should be to gain some practical experience which will help you in the implementation of your project. The intention of this step is to enable you to become familiar with the capabilities of some of the more common software types and, as an additional benefit, you will start to become familiar with some of the ideas and concepts involved in the use of microcomputers. Importantly, you will start to gain a familiarity with some of the limitations of microcomputers. This newly acquired knowledge will stand you in good stead as far as your own project is concerned and also it will help you to withstand the onslaught of jargon that is the norm of advertising material and salespeople. Probably the easiest starting-point will be to become familiar with a word processor and then with either a database or spreadsheet package. Time permitting, it would be sensible at this point to try more than one package of each type so that your perceptions of the capabilities of a particular software type are not predicated solely upon the functionality available from a single product. It would be preferable if you could achieve this experience by using other people's equipment so that you are free to purchase equipment after you have been through this step.

You should now be in a position to begin the process of selecting the hardware and software which you will use for the project. A detailed discussion of the process of software selection appears later in this chapter. A generally accepted rule is that you should select the software before the hardware; that is to say, software selection should not be determined by the hardware but, rather, the hardware should be chosen because it is the most suitable hardware on which to run the chosen software. However sensible and widely accepted this rule may be, you should recognize that there will be situations in which it cannot be implemented. If your library or, even, the wider organization has a policy on microcomputer purchase, you may find that this restricts your choice of software. Increasingly, large organizations will operate lists of approved software as well as of approved hardware. It would be as well to explore any such policy before you proceed further. Does it mean that you can go outside the recommended list if you can make an acceptable case, or does it mean that you can only purchase from the approved list? Whilst the strict imposition of a restricted list of approved software may mean that the project is developed on a less-than-perfect software base, you can take comfort from the fact that the task of software evaluation is simplified to one of examining those products on the approved list.

This could be a considerable simplification of this step. Furthermore, it is likely that the availability of a large pool of expertise in the use of an approved package will be of considerable benefit.

Two points emerge from the preceding discussion which are worth amplification. The first is that no piece of software will be perfect for any project unless it is written specifically for that project; this is an approach which is likely to be prohibitively expensive. The corollary of this is that in any project it is likely that the solution will, to some degree, be amended from the proposed solution because of the capabilities of the software chosen. The second is to emphasize that it is important to seek help when you need it. Generally speaking, all microcomputer users are tremendous enthusiasts and are only too pleased to help other users. In addition, you are likely to get some advice from organizational 'computer centres', other librarians and, on occasions, software suppliers. However, do not expect much support from your software supplier unless that is part of the contract and/or you have a particularly good working relationship with them. An important point is to have the problem clearly understood and expressed before help is sought. As you become more experienced you should be prepared to help others who seek advice from you. There is an element of equity about this suggestion since it is not unreasonable to provide help as well as to receive it. Moreover, it is highly likely that by the process of offering help you will also benefit yourself.

It is important that you are realistic about the commitment of time which will be necessary to implement a solution suitable for your chosen project. Do not be misled by the glib advertisements which imply that a particular software package will revolutionize your working practices within minutes of being lifted out of its box. It is likely that many pieces of software have the capacity to have a considerable, and positive, impact on your work; however, for that to occur, it will be necessary to invest a considerable amount of time. Effort must be expended both in understanding how a package works and then in implementing a solution to the particular problem. One suggestion which has been made is that the most pessimistic estimate should be made of time necessary to implement each stage of a project and then the estimate should be doubled. This is a sensible precaution in order to prevent you from becoming downhearted at apparently slow progress and to disillusion others who may have unrealistic expectations of the speed with which a piece of software can be learned and utilized. The words of warning regarding the time commitment may sound gloomy, and it is only reasonable to add that it is almost certain that you will gain a considerable amount of enjoyment and satisfaction as the application is developed.

A final point is that it would be sensible to have a test, or pilot, solution to the problem. This will enable you to see how a problem may be solved and to observe the consequences of some of the decisions taken before you progress too far in the particular application. Do not be afraid to modify your solution as a result of this trial run.

6.3 Software identification

The obvious first step in software choice is to make a detailed analysis of the products of a particular type available. There are numerous sources of information which can be searched to locate potential software tools. Firstly, many of the microcomputer magazines, such as *Practical computing, Personal computer world* and *Personal computer magazine*, regularly carry reviews of software products, advertisements and listings of products available. In addition, many of the more technologically orientated of the library and information science journals will be helpful sources of information. Such periodicals as *Library software review, Special libraries, Information processing and management* and *Online review*, amongst others, often provide useful information.

More comprehensive listings of software available and other information can be identified by looking at general software directories and more specialized sources, such as the *World information technology manual*, edited by A. E. Cawkell, and the *Business software directory*, the fourth edition of which was published by Learned Information in 1991. In addition, there are some examples of well-established directories of particular software types which may be productive sources of information. The best-established of these is *Text retrieval*, originally edited by C. D. Hamilton, the third edition of which was revised by Robert Kimberley and J. E. Rowley and published by Gower in 1990; another example is offered by the *Directory of expert system tools*, edited by A. Morris and A. Reed and published by Learned Information. Another good source is Hilary Dyer's *Directory of library and information retrieval software for microcomputers*, the fourth revised edition having been edited by Alison Gunson and published by Gower in 1990. In addition to printed sources, the use of online databases should not be overlooked in the search for potential software products.

The well-established exhibitions attached to various conferences are frequently fruitful sources of information about potential software solutions. The exhibition associated with the International Online Information Meeting at Olympia, each December, is probably the largest of these events and will provide a good opportunity to see a wide range of text retrieval software. The annual Library Technology Fair at the University of Hertfordshire is becoming a useful event to visit regularly and the Library Resources Exhibition in June, at Birmingham, is growing rapidly. More general exhibitions of microcomputer software may also repay a visit.

6.4 Software evaluation

The criteria to be applied when selecting a piece of software can be thought of as a combination of the general characteristics to be considered when purchasing any type of software and the aspects which will be specific to a software type and the particular application. It is not feasible to list aspects for all software types discussed in this book and so in this section of the chapter the general characteristics are considered and, as an example, the particular aspects which might be considered when purchasing text retrieval software are outlined. Before evaluating any software, it may be useful to consider the development of a standard form, or checklist, so that each of the candidate packages is treated in the same manner, which will help in the comparison of alternatives.

General characteristics which should be taken into account in the evaluation of any package are discussed in the succeeding paragraphs. A clear understanding of the hardware and software requirements for the package to operate is important. For example, it is important to determine the minimum size of memory and the versions of DOS, or other operating system, which the package requires. For any large application, particularly a database application, it is sensible to have in mind a likely size to which the application may grow and to calculate the storage requirements, and then to ensure that a hard disc with sufficient spare capacity is available. Furthermore, it is wise to ensure that the version of the package which is being offered to you is the latest available and that an upgrade is not likely to be brought out in the next few months.

Increasingly, packages provide mechanisms for importing from, and exporting data to, other packages. Sometimes this is a matter of data compatibility with another package of the same type, such as those database packages which offer compatibility with dBase files because it is the market leader in microcomputer database management systems. But it is also often important to be able to import and export data between a package and packages of completely different types. For example, the expert system shell Crystal readily facilitates the exchange of data with dBase and Lotus 1-2-3 and it is possible to use the package in combination with a memory resident hypertext package in a manner which is relatively 'seamless'; that is to say, the user does not know when the move between the different pieces of software has occurred. So the availability, and ease, of importing and exporting data between packages should be investigated if it is felt to be relevant.

The ease of use of the package is an important consideration. Different users have varying notions of what constitutes an easy-to-use piece of software but some general points can be made. The layout on the screen should not be cluttered. It is all too easy to put too much information on to a single screen. Any system of on-screen guidance, whether from prompts about what to do next, or from the labelling of fields, needs to be achieved in as straightforward and jargon-free manner as possible. Colour is now taken for granted in the design of systems but it must be used in a careful manner so that there are not too many different hues on the screen at any one time. Colours can be used to guide the user in the operation of the system by careful and consistent use between screens. There are potentially useful opportunities for using colours such as red and green – which have obvious associations with 'danger' and 'safe to proceed' – in ways which indicate, for example, that taking a particular course of action would delete a file (using red) or cause a non-destructive action to occur (using green). The error messages should be comprehensible to inexperienced users. This means that they should be presented in the language best understood by the user and, wherever possible, should offer some explanation of the error and the available options. If an aural signal such as a 'bleep' is used, this should be discreet and readily capable of being silenced. If it is appropriate, there should be access to context-sensitive 'help' screens, built into the software, which will offer guidance on how to proceed in the given situation. Fortunately there has been considerable progress with respect to making systems more usable in recent years. An obvious example is the interaction which is possible on most CD-ROM systems which is considerably greater than with remote search services.

Mention of comprehensibility leads, almost naturally, to some consideration of documentation. In many cases its presentation and content have improved considerably over recent years. However, there are still cases where the maxim 'written by idiots for use by geniuses' applies and so it is important to ensure that the package chosen is one which is supplied with good-quality documentation. The quality element refers to the information contained in the manual, its organization and indexing, and its physical presentation. It may also be useful to determine what, if any, support is available from the software supplier. Suppliers of specialized software, such as that for text retrieval and expert system shells, may be more likely to offer after-sales support and help lines, even if only on registration and payment of a fee, than are suppliers of standard office automation packages, such as spreadsheets and file handlers. To some extent this after-sales service justifies the larger costs which these packages generally attract.

The cost of the package should be taken into account. If it is considerably different from other packages of the type then it becomes important to find out why this is so. If it is more expensive, is the extra cost purchasing additional functionality, usability or support from the supplier? It may simply be providing a bigger profit margin for either the software company or your supplier. If the package is selling at a much lower price than the norm for similar software, then it is important to be aware of why this is the case. It may not be a sensible action to purchase an apparent bargain if the price has been considerably reduced because the package has lost market share and its future is in doubt, or a major update is imminent. The relative importance of cost and the other criteria will vary from application to application.

In order to demonstrate the type and level of package-specific criteria which should be considered, the case of text retrieval software for a text database will be considered. Some of the features mentioned will be more important than others for a particular application and it may be judicious to label facilities as either essential or desirable so that the options available are discussed in a structured manner. Search facilities should include:

the ability to search on a specified field;
the ability to search for individual words within a field;
the ability to use Boolean operators AND, OR and NOT;
the ability to use truncation;
the ability to use wildcards within words;
the ability to specify term-positional criteria.

An intending purchaser should also consider:

If term-positional criteria can be used, by what means is this achieved, given the varying approaches available?
Is it possible to retrieve on unindexed terms (for example, by string searching)?
Are the search commands clear and unambiguous?
Is it possible to access an online thesaurus?

Required input facilities might include:

ability to input from tape, disk, keyboard or downloaded data from online databases;
a range of indexing options (for example, automatic indexing of all words or selective indexing of all words);
the ability to specify a stopword list;
the ability to store a thesaurus, maintaining term relationships.

Required output facilities might include:

the ability to send output to screen, printer or disk;
the ability to define record layout;
the ability to send output to a word processor for further editing;
the ability to sort output by desired features.

6.5 Sources of information and advice

There is no sense in conducting a software evaluation in a vacuum and thereby ignoring the experiences of others. This is particularly true if it is possible to identify people who have used a candidate software package in a manner similar to the proposed application. Thus, other users should be an important source of advice since they will have had experience of a package in operation. This experience may offer insight and indications of limitations which are more realistic than the descriptions of software in advertisements or glossy presentations by salespeople. Some packages, in particular those text retrieval packages which operate in both a mainframe and a microcomputer environment, have well-established user groups. Groups such as the Crystal User Group (an expert system shell) or the STATUS User Group (text retrieval software) can be useful sources of advice and serve as central points for contacting other users.

In the United Kingdom, the Library and Information Technology Centre at South Bank University, London, acts as a centre for advice and information on the library applications of information technology. It may be a fruitful source of advice on particular software packages, on how to get started with a particular project, and for information about users of a particular package. Professional groupings, such as the Information Technology Group of the Library Association, may also provide useful contacts or sources of advice.

Many software houses will make available trial, or demonstration, disks which can be helpful in demonstrating the facilities available with a given piece of software. Sometimes these are available free; other companies may charge a nominal fee such as £50.00. A free disk may be little more than an on-screen advertisement or, at best, give only limited help; a simple application built with the package, for example. Demonstration packages should give a clear indication of the facilities available in the full package. A more helpful approach is for the demonstration package to contain a full manual and to allow full functionality so that the capabilities of the package can be explored. However, these disks usually place some restriction on the size of the application which can be developed. For example, the demonstration package for a piece of database software may only permit a database of up to fifty items to be created. In some cases the software house will reduce the price of the full package, if bought, by the cost of the demonstration package.

The search for the most appropriate software package may be aided by attending product review sessions at conferences or at local meetings of organizations such as online user groups. Direct contact with the software house may sometimes be productive. Whilst it is necessary to remember that all sales personnel are concerned with selling their own product, in the case of the more specialized products – such as text retrieval software and expert systems shells – the approach is usually not 'hard sell' and it may be possible to glean useful information and advice.

Nevertheless, at the end of the day, regardless of the amount of advice which is available, it will be necessary to take the plunge, order software and start on your projected application. In making your decision you should remember that:

- You will only find a piece of software which fits your requirements exactly if you have it programmed for your specific application. Thus you should expect to have to make some compromises to fit the capabilities of the most appropriate software available.
- The only way in which you will really learn how to use a piece of software is to buy it and develop an application. You can be certain that you will make mistakes, learn a lot, enjoy yourself (sometimes!) and, it is to be hoped, develop a useful application.
- There is no point in buying any piece of software if you are not able, or prepared, to set aside time to read the manuals, experiment and learn to use it. Even the most 'user-friendly' package needs this level of attention if you are to make the best use of it.

If you are in charge of a software development project, make sure that plenty of time is included for evaluation and becoming familiar with the software. This is especially important if you or other members of the project team will have the responsibility of training others. Nothing serves to demoralize intending users more quickly than a trainer who is constantly surprised by the way in which the software package behaves.

It is also useful to keep a record of experiences and problems with the software. Such is the complexity of modern software that it is rarely feasible (and some computational theorists suggest, impossible) to validate software completely. Reputable software developers will have subjected software to an extensive range of tests and will have discovered and corrected many errors. The product, when released, should work effectively and efficiently but may still include undiscovered errors, or 'bugs', which only affect the operation of the program in unusual circumstances. It may be your fate to discover one of these, in which case the first resort is to contact the supplier who will usually be prepared to sort out the problem. A record of such problems can provide the supplier with a starting-point for tracking down the cause of the problem. Such a record may also reveal misunderstanding by users of the purpose and use of some of the commands and functions of the software. Again, this may be of some help to suppliers in the rewriting of documentation or on-screen 'help' pages.

Evaluation is often seen as the final step in implementing a system and the task of introducing a new software package is no exception. A thorough record of problems encountered with the software will serve as a useful guide when contemplating future purchases, especially if some opinion of the helpfulness of the supplier in dealing with these problems has also been recorded. It is also helpful to keep a list of desirable features or functions which seem to be lacking in the package in use. This will also help when planning to select the successor to an existing package.

Finally, the project manager should remember that there is only one purpose in implementing a new system or in improving an existing system: that is, to help users. The views of users, their comments, criticisms and problems in using a system should be carefully considered. Some will arise, perhaps, from misunderstandings or a failure to appreciate the use of some feature of a system. What this may be revealing is not a blithe disregard for instructions or an inability to understand but, rather, a point at which additional, or better, instruction and guidance is needed. Such comments may also, however, reveal dissatisfaction with the system for justifiable reasons. Whilst it may not be immediately possible to rectify such apparent faults, it will do much for good relations with users if they are made aware that their comments have been noted and may lead, in the future, to an improved design. No system is ever perfect, no design is ever final.

INDEX

The basics of data management for information services

logic, positional *see* positional logic

Macintosh *see* Apple Macintosh
microcomputers
macros
  word processing 80–1
mailmerging software 83
management of projects *see* project
  management
management of resources *see*
  resource management
management information systems 4
managerial roles 5–6
managers, file *see* file managers
memory devices
  disks 20–1, 27–8
  Random Access Memory 16
mice
  input devices 17–18
microcomputers
  communication ports 16–17
  configurations 6
  *Directory of library and
  information retrieval software
  for microcomputers* 104–5
  disks 20–1
  environmental aspects 26–7
  input devices 18–20
  memory 16
  modems 21–2
  network links 22
  output devices 18–20
  processor types 15–16
  see also computer systems,
  hardware, software
MIS *see* management information
  systems
models, data *see* data models
modems 21–2
Morris, A. 104
multi–tasking 9–10

network analysis

project management software 87–8
networks
  Local Area Networks 22
  telecommunications 8
normal forms
  data models 74
normalization
  data models 74–6
Norton, N. P. 1, 11

online information retrieval see
  information retrieval
Online review
  software identification 104
operating systems 22–23
outliner programs 86–7
output devices
  displays 18–19
  printers 19–20, 47

packages, software *see* software
parallel ports 16
PC *see* IBM PC microcomputers
peripherals *see* input devices,
  memory devices, output devices
Personal computer magazine
  software identification 104
Personal computer world magazine
  software identification 104
personal computers *see* microcomputers
personal reference management
  software 67–9
PERT *see* Programme Evaluation
  Review Technique
phonetic matching
  information retrieval 66–7
'pop–ups'
  word processing 78, 83, 87
ports
  communication ports 16–17
positional logic
  information retrieval 66–7

power supplies
computer equipment 26–7
Practical computing magazine
software identification 104
printers
carriage width 19, 47, 88
types 19–20
printing
database records 59–60
desk-top publishing 86
project management software
output 88
spreadsheet data 47–8, 51
word–processed text 79
Programme Evaluation Review
Technique
project management software 87–8
programs *see* software
project coordinator
role 12–13, 26
terms of reference 13–14
project management
hardware selection 102
importance of documentation 14
project objectives 101
role of coordinator 12–13
security of system 27–9
software for 87–8
software evaluation 105–8
software identification 104–5
software selection 102–4
steps in 101–4, 110–11
public domain software 24
publishing, desk-top *see* desk-top
publishing

quorum function searching 69–70

RAM *see* Random Access Memory
Random Access Memory 16
Reed, A. 104
reference, terms of
see terms of reference

resource management
use of spreadsheets 52–3
roles
librarians and information workers
1–2
managers 5–6
project coordinators 12–13
Rowley, J. E. 104

scanners
input devices 18
searching
information retrieval 61–5, 69–70
security
disk failure 27–8, 46
spreadsheet features 45–7
utility programs 28
viruses 28–9
serial ports 16
shareware software 24
Shell International Petroleum
expert system application 91
shelving capacity
use of spreadsheets 52–3
software
acquisition 23–4
advice centres 108–9
applications in general 23–4
Business software directory 104
care in purchasing 14, 110–11
costs 107
databases 54–76
demonstrations 109–10
desk-top publishing 85–6
documentation 107
evaluation procedures 105–8, 111
expert systems 88–97
hypermedia 97–100
identification 104–5
installation 29–31
integrated packages 24–5
Library software review 104
'made to measure' systems 26